Sacred Flow

Discovering Life in the Divine Current

MISSIONAL PRESS

Smyrna, DE

Jason, Pleasure, meeting you. Live Freely in His Flow!

Artie Sposaro

A.7.S.

Visit Missional Press's website at www.missional-press.com.

Missional Press
149 Golden Plover Dr.
Smyrna, DE 19977

ISBN 10: 0-9825719-7-6
ISBN 13: 978-0-9825719-7-2

Printed in the United States of America

For Elizabeth, Lydia, Lincoln, and Elgin.

Acknowledgements

This book began its germination over ten years ago. Scores of people have been a part of my life through those years. I sincerely appreciate those *many* people who've befriended me and invested in me along the way.

Specifically related to this book, several friends were invaluable. Thanks to Rob Eagar, Joseph Goodson, Ash Zook, and Charles Spoelstra. These friends regularly offered feedback, wise counsel, and genuine encouragement. I wouldn't have started, stayed the course, or finished without them. A special thanks to Carole Spencer at George Fox Seminary who guided, edited, and encouraged my research and writing during my doctoral work. Thanks also to Len Sweet, Loren Kerns, Chuck Conniry, and my classmates at George Fox. Their influence substantially enriched my research and writing. Thanks to Roger Balko and Nancy Talero for their creativity expressed in the book's cover. Thanks to Garrett Brown for the watermarked design at the front and back of the book. Many thanks to David Phillips and Missional Press for publishing *Sacred Flow* and to my editor Rocky Moore for bringing more order and readability to the text.

Thanks to my mom who, while I was growing up (and even now) wouldn't allow me to say "*I can't*" and to my dad whose work ethic rubbed off on me, at least a little bit. Finally, thanks to my wife, Elizabeth, who bore my incessant insecurity, very rough drafts, constant note taking, verbal rambling, and absence. Her endless grace, patience, and feedback allowed this book to happen and significantly shaped it.

I truly appreciate you all.

Preface

Before you begin, I feel it's imperative that I share with you that I'm not writing as a weathered spiritual guru. I don't live in a monastery, cave, desert, castle, or anywhere else considered spiritually hip. I'm a late 30s believer, seeker, pilgrim, husband, dad, brother, son, friend, leader, teacher, learner, reader, writer, pastor, counselor, and coach. I believe I'm an everyman of sorts, and normal for the most part (whatever that means). I've lived in the United States and abroad. I've followed Jesus inside and outside of the institutional church. I've roamed both academic halls and athletic fields. I've worked with for-profits and non-profits. I've spent time on organizational boards and snowboards. I've experienced plenty of highs and lows and walked through them with others. Most significantly, I've spent the past ten years or so earnestly wrestling with what it means to live in the flow of God's Spirit. I've been intentional about opening my soul's eyes to a broader view of Christian faith, more specifically what it might mean to wholly trust God and be divinely empowered in each moment. This book doesn't intend to produce a new spiritual method or system, but to offer a perspective of Christian spirituality that resurrects or simply inspires your everyday faith. I hope these pages articulate a message of living with God that thoroughly resonates with you. I pray that sacred flow reorients, revolutionizes, and empowers your faith in ways you never dreamed possible…it did mine.

Sacred Flow
Discovering Life in the Divine Current

Introduction: Finding Flow   1

The First Current: Foundation for Sacred Flow

1: Religious Woes or a Faith That Flows?   9

2: Dive into the Flow   21

3: Jesus Flows   35

4: The Flow Within   49

5: Our Freedom to Flow   63

The Second Current: Framing a Faith That Flows

6: Focus   77

7: Challenge   89

8: Feedback   101

9: The Inward Fruits   113

10: The Outward Fruits   125

The Third Current: Daily Faith in the Flow

11: Flow-Ready Faith   139

12: Living Into the Sacred Flow   151

Benediction   165

Appendix: Practicing Grace   169

Bibliography   179

Notes   187

Introduction

Finding Flow

Open yourself to God without measure. Let His
life flow through you like a torrent. Fear nothing on
the road you are walking. God will lead you by the hand.
Let your love for Him cast out the fear you feel for yourself.
Francois Fenelon

What if your life could be more enjoyable and require less effort? What if you could tap into God's strength in everyday life so that you wouldn't have to strain along in your strength? What if you could live so intimately with God that you regularly make molehills out of mountains instead of vice versa? This is not only possible; it's the way you're meant to live. You're meant to live in the flow of God's Spirit.

In reality, daily life easily drains us. We often find ourselves in a passionless haze slogging through our days. The spirituality meant to buoy us actually contributes weight. Our stuck-ness reflects a *supernatural* faith that is too grounded in the *natural*. We minimize or altogether neglect intimate relationship with the mysterious *super*. This inattention leads to our sense of disconnection with God's life in ours. Without this vital connection we are left to our own power and (de)vices.

The result is earthliness. Notice, I didn't say *earthiness*. Our spirituality could use plenty more *earthiness* – rooted authenticity. Earthliness refers to what Medieval English mystic Julian of Norwich called *oblivio Dei,* obliviousness to God's presence and power. Even in our spirituality we ignore God. I know all about *oblivio Dei*; I've lived it most my life. Many of us have.

1

Growing up, I attended church regularly rarely missing a Sunday. My childhood church-going took place at the Catholic Church. Living as a Catholic in the suburbs of the Deep South outside of Atlanta in the 1980s made me atypical, and the evangelistic target of local Southern Baptists. In high school I actually merged my Catholicism with the Southern Baptists. I've not met another person whose Sunday schedule shaped up like mine. I attended special masses, meetings, and events at the Catholic Church as well as youth events and multiple services at a local Baptist church.

In college I continued broadening my religious horizons by majoring in Religion, sporadically attending a Presbyterian Church, hanging out at the Baptist Center, and helping lead a non-denominational campus fellowship. I attended Bible study, led a Bible study, and volunteered at a homeless ministry. By my senior year, my schedule was completely overrun with religious activity. After college I started a Master of Divinity program at an Associate Reformed Presbyterian seminary and later graduated from a Baptist seminary.

You might think that with this much religious intensity and denominational diversity I would have been spiritually satisfied...not even close. Ritualistic religion became my life's rhythm. In the midst of my full-on religious sprint, I tired. Misinterpreting Paul's encouragement to run the race of faith, I was hyperventilating in the race of religion. Functioning primarily in my own strength, I couldn't measure up to the expectations, standards, and morals that I perceived God laid on me or those I laid upon myself. My spiritual cycle consisted of trying hard to please God and others, failing consistently, begging God's forgiveness, berating myself, wallowing in shame, building resolve, and trying again.

Religion was killing me.

To be clear, when I say *religion* I am not alluding to the church, a body of faith-filled people. Nor am I referring to a grace-saturated organic relationship with God characterized by living, moving, and being in him. But I am speaking of a performance-based spirit, approach, or system that's supposed to bring me closer to the divine standard and God himself. We typically call this way of life religious legalism.

My religiosity crushed my soul to the point that I began losing hope that Christianity could supply any substantial measure of contentment. Jesus was great, but religion had beaten me down. I had spent most of my short life striving for God and I was left wanting. A particular lyric in a song by the band U2 resonated with me,

"You [Jesus] broke the bonds and you loosed the chains, carried the cross of my shame, of my shame, you know I believe it, but I still haven't found what I'm looking for."[1]

Maybe you sense something *more* has to be out there, but you feel the same lack of fulfillment. You earnestly work at your faith but feel beaten down and inadequate. You secretly fear that the *more* to life with God you seek simply doesn't exist. You've given religion your all and still experience little flow, freedom, empowerment, peace, joy, or intimacy.

Religion is not the answer.

We're meant for more. We're destined to experience life beyond religion. We're meant to live freely in God's Spirit, intimately walking with God and tenaciously trusting in his love. God means to dislodge our faith, set us free in the flow of his divine current. In this book, we will explore what it means to tap into God's sacred flow and transform religion run aground into faith that flows.

why sacred flow?

Most of us have some experience with flow. The flow experience is an oasis characterized by fluid connection with whatever we are doing and everything surrounding us. To describe flow we typically use the colloquial expression *the zone.* Our culture has supplied various idioms to describe flow, such as: *unconscious, locked in, in the bubble, complete satisfaction, focused, totally involved, peaceful, autopilot, everything clicks, en fuego, switched on, ideal, nothing else matters, in the groove, unbeatable, super alive, floating, weightless, total control, detached, wholeness, optimal pace, and tuned in* to name a few.[2] All of us have likely experienced flow at some level through a competition, intense conversation, absorption in work, or while engaging in a hobby. While flowing, both our sense of self-consciousness and self-effort fade. We float; totally engrossed in our activity. A flowing faith embodies these same characteristics.

The term *sacred* can mean many things. In this book, I am referring to sacred as divine, spiritual, holy, or godly. The "sacred" in *sacred flow* aims to expand the psychological or humanistic aspects flow to include the divine. It weaves what has been considered secular into the sacred. Flow becomes vital to our orientation and intimate connection with God and everyday life. Sacred flow is holistic flow. It encompasses the spiritual, physical, mental, and emotional.

Sacred Flow offers hope by using flow as a both a powerful metaphor and a framework, presenting Christian spirituality as life flowing within the divine current. As an image or metaphor, flow offers the Christian faith as fluid-like *unbroken continuity* with God. Sacred flow inspires a faith that is characterized by continuous intimate connection with God.

As a framework, flow leads us into the rhythm of God's Spirit through *focus, challenge,* and *feedback*. These three components serve as the roots of flow and Christian spirituality. Sacred flow integrates recent peak-experience psychological research with two-millennium old Christianity. Sacred flow reconnects Christianity with its ancient past and repositions it for the future.

In order to effectively establish and express this idea, *Sacred Flow* is arranged into three sections or currents. The first current, *Foundation for Sacred Flow,* describes how religious legalism has stagnated our faith. It introduces and expounds flow and how Jesus' life modeled what it means to live in the divine current. Lastly, this section establishes how followers of Jesus may flow with God as Jesus did.

The second current, *Framing a Faith That Flows,* builds on this foundation to express Christianity through the framework of flow. This section explains how Christian spirituality integrates with flow's roots and fruits. It fully integrates a life of faith with the fundamentals of flow. The final current, *Daily Faith in the Flow,* folds sacred flow's foundation and framework into our daily life. This section includes a chapter that introduces a flow-ready soul posture, a chapter with practical talk about living into the sacred flow, and a benediction that ushers us out into the sacred flow. Finally, this current concludes with an appendix called *Practicing Grace* that revisits many spiritual disciplines with reference to sacred flow.

Sacred flow balances the mystical and practical, embracing and encouraging both, promoting an active Christian spirituality absorbed *in* and empowered *by* God's indwelling presence. It keeps us vitally connected with God's mysterious grace and the world we live in every day. Sacred flow offers a way of Christian living guided by the Spirit rather than by institution, religious doctrine, dogma, values, morals, principles, and standards. The latter have their place but mustn't occupy the center of our faith.

Nothing short of a revolution has occurred in my faith. I approach life in a completely different manner than I did before being swept away in God's flow. Tapping into sacred flow has connected me with the way of Jesus, aligning me with God's presence and inviting his participation in every aspect of my life. I no longer spend most of my time self-consumed, concerned if I am measuring up. *Am I doing enough? Being enough? Am I proving my love for God today? Is God going to be disappointed with me again today?* What a remarkable freedom I'm realizing. I've shaken loose from religious muck into a powerful current. As I face muddy, intense, complex, tragic, or ugly circumstances in my daily life, I look to the Spirit's flow to love, teach, empower, and guide in and through me.

Are you stuck, lacking flow? Are you dissatisfied with life? Are you worn out by life or religious legalism and longing to authentically experience God? Are you enjoying your life…with God? Have you lost (or ever found) any sense of flow with God, or him flowing through you?

Sacred Flow invites you to ebb and flow in God's Spirit. It encourages an intense intimacy with God that makes loving God and others come more naturally. You can't escape the harsh realities of life, but you can deal with them differently. As life brings you difficult challenges you can flow through them. You can look to Christ with you, in you, and through you to make things happen. You can learn trust the *super* in the *natural* moment by moment.

I pray that *Sacred Flow* dislodges any stuck-ness in your faith, releasing you to dive deeply and swim freely in God's graceful flow. I sincerely hope that God will draw you into his divine current in ways you've never even imagined.

The First Current

Foundation for Sacred Flow

*current: (noun) - the flow of electricity or power.
The steady, smooth movement of a large portion of
air, body of water, etc.*

1

Religious Woes or a Faith That Flows?

> If Christianity is to be renewed, this can be brought
> about only by a return to its root; that means to
> Revelation. We must place ourselves before this, must put
> aside all preconceived ideas, all portraits of art, all habitual
> attitudes, and must open our souls, perceive with our
> inner ear, behold with our inner eye, word upon word,
> in Matthew and Mark and Luke, in Paul and John.
> *Romano Guardini*

As a weary Christian in my mid-twenties, I was too embarrassed to admit the troubled state of my soul. I knew there had to be a more meaningful way to experience my faith. If God were real, the living creator and sustainer of all things, the one who gave himself into humanity, then why did my spirituality boil off to try, try harder, and never give up? For God's sake and my own, I had been plotting, strategizing, straining, managing, arranging, succeeding, failing, burning out, and repeating the process. My faith was stuck in a fruitless paradigm. Like the condemned mythological king Sisyphus, I felt that I was endlessly straining to push a boulder up a steep hill only to watch it roll down again.

Sisyphus' plight characterizes my faith back then, and describes Christian spirituality for many of us today. This *Sisyphus system* defines and undermines not only our spiritual lives, but also our lives in general. Where is our rock today? Should we be pushing it farther, faster, or harder? Are we following biblically inspired rock-pushing principles? Or have we given up pushing altogether…for now? Over time there becomes little difference between being atop the mountain and being run over by the boulder as it returns to the valley.

The Sisyphus system results in a sickness, the Sisyphus syndrome, which has infected most of our culture. Its bacterial strain is called "try harder." It's everywhere in society, from daycares to assisted living facilities, from schools to top companies. It infects practically everything and everyone. Christianity has a bad case of the Sisyphus syndrome. We pay lip service to empowering grace but live by true grit. Trying and trying harder is how we are told we will become and remain good mature children of God. This age-old lie, first told just before humanity's fall from grace, permeates today's Christian culture. It's not just hidden within the hard-line fundamentalist or ultra-progressive camps. It's scattered throughout churches occupying the mainstream and the fringes. It's intentionally and unintentionally, subtly and not so subtly propagated across the spectrum. It's coming from pulpits and prayers, fellowship halls and evangelism calls, from mentoring meetings and Sunday morning greetings. We hear it in our worship lyrics and in conversations along the winding hallways of our churches. It's everywhere.

> **How sad that millions of human beings are dead to God's harmonious rhythm, that they live lives so deprived of this joyful, childlike abandonment to the divine source of all life.**
> *George A. Maloney*

The Sisyphus syndrome has us perpetually running on a steep grade spiritual treadmill while pushing a massive rock. Regrettably, we are running in place, getting nowhere. Soul-sweat pools as we hold out hope that we're getting spiritually fit and that this workout will end before serious injury incurs. Inevitably, we collapse, smacking a knee, elbow, face, or all of the above while being aggressively flung to the ground. We lie there ashamed and in pain until we muster the strength to stand, limp, walk, and then run again…all the while hoping no one saw our embarrassing collapse.

Thankfully, a cure exists for the Sisyphus system and its resulting syndrome. It's God's grace. God's grace is readily available, easily accessible, and in endless supply. Christianity is not about pushing rocks or treadmill trying. Authentic

Christianity leads us off the treadmill hill altogether into a grace-filled divine current. It leads us to a God-empowered way of being and doing. This Sisyphus-less way began flooding my soul through a simple question.

Are you living for God or from God?

This pithy little question broke my soul's dam. It's an unsophisticated question with profound implications. These were the first words mouthed by a speaker at a conference I attended many years ago. He went on to say that the only way to live *for* God is to live *from* God. This doesn't refer to living far away *from* God but rather being empowered *by* God. We are meant to employ God's strength, not simply our own. This way of life unfolds the gift of the gospel in our daily life. Paul, writing to the Christian community in Galatia, encapsulates what it means to live *from* God when he says, "I have been crucified with Christ. I myself no longer live, but Christ lives in me. So I live my life in this earthly body by trusting in the Son of God, who loved me and gave himself for me."[3]

The Christian life is about Christ living in and through us…our part is to continually and completely trust him to do so. This is not to suggest that we are mere puppets. We are unique divinely empowered people. The love of God means to flow through us!

Maybe this idea of living *from* God has always been obvious to you, but to me it was nothing short of divine revelation. Yes, I had read this verse of Scripture – *Christ lives in me* – before and many others like it countless times, but their true weight never really registered until that moment. This simple question and its implications caused my heart to resonate with conviction, grief, and resurrection. Finally, paradise lost had found me. My soul sighed with relief and jumped with joy. Living *from* God presented a new way of being with God. It would move me from rote religion to something truly relational, spiritual, dynamic, and rhythmic.

With this renewal came an unexpected integration. A few months later, I was randomly surfing sports psychology websites. In my skimming I ran across a page detailing the characteristic fruits of flow. I discovered that flow had been researched for decades and that this study had gleaned some really fascinating results. While flowing, people reported experiencing a universal set of effects – what you feel when you flow. They sensed a supernatural union with their surroundings, self-validation, authentic identity, absorption into their activity, inner peace, effortlessness, a sense of control, selflessness, timelessness, and emotional balance. Remarkably, life in my newfound grace-filled paradigm was producing these same fruits. I came to the realization that Christianity gives full expression to flow and vice versa. We are meant to experience flow and its fruits in our faith. *Epiphany.*

Christianity flows!

reorienting rhythm and flow

This book's title or the content on the back cover likely stirred in you some apprehension along with interest. This wariness may be because we don't typically associate the concept of flow, living in rhythm with God, or discovering life in the divine current with "orthodox" Christian faith. Google *spiritual rhythm, divine current,* or *flow* and see how many references to Christian spirituality you find. Very few. These concepts are most commonly used within the contexts of the Eastern Religions and the New Age movement. Therefore, in order to transform our faith from a religion into a sacred flow, I need to reorient *rhythm* and *flow* more comfortably within the Christian experience.

Rhythm and flow aren't copyrighted by other faith traditions. We sorely need them. They bring freshness to our Christ-following. To be a follower is to be a learner, a disciple, an apprentice, an astute flow-er. God longs for us to discover his rhythm and experience his flow.

The word rhythm from the Greek *rhythmus* or *rhythmos* means, "movement in time" or "measured flow." Rhythm is movement with a patterned recurrence (flow) of elements beats, accents, motifs, themes, etc. that occur in regular or irregular intervals.[4] Have you ever been in an elevator and the soft instrumental music you hear sounds familiar but you can't seem to place it? Then it hits you; it's Bruce Springsteen as elevator

> **We are oscillatory beings in an oscillatory universe. Rhythmicity is our inheritance.**
> *Jim Loehr & Tony Schwartz*

music! Sorry Boss. There were no lyrics but the song's rhythm –
its particular repeated pattern of beats was recognizable to you.
Similarly, if your favorite song were playing right now, you
would naturally begin moving to its rhythm - tapping, swaying,
humming, or singing. You would naturally adjust your
movement to match the rhythm of the song.

As humans we are always in motion. Our spirit, soul,
and body undulate constantly. We rhythmically move though
we don't often recognize it. Some of us struggle with rhythm
and have difficulty matching beats, themes, etc. whether it's
music or spirituality. Nonetheless, we still possess rhythm and
are moved by those things that resonate within us.

God initiates and sustains rhythm (and flow) for
everything. God not only moves rhythmically, he brings us into
his rhythm and injects his rhythm into us. This gives great
affirmation to those who groove with God naturally and hope to
us who are rhythmically challenged. We simply need to give our
full attention to discovering and moving in step with God's beat.
It greatly benefits us to regularly stop in the midst of our frenetic
days and take a few deep prayerful breaths in order re-attune
ourselves with God's peaceful rhythm.

God's rhythm, his recurring theme, accent, and
heartbeat is love. God is love. Therefore, love is the core ideal of
Christianity and sacred flow. Often God's love seems erratic,
lacking any pattern whatsoever. We are loved and led to love in
ways that don't seem to reflect God having rhythm. In truth, the
complexity of God's inexplicable love-rhythm invites us into to a
deeper trust and results in a textured harmony far beyond
anything we could create otherwise. Leaning into God's
mysterious rhythm we continually ask, "Father, how are you
loving me and leading me to love right here, right now?"

Rhythm and flow are closely related. Rhythm's first
cousin is the Latin term, *rhein,* which means, "to flow."[5] Being in
rhythm leads us to deeper connection, unbroken continuity,
flow. Rhythm serves as a precursor to flow. As we continually
and fully engage in our activities, flow happens, especially when
our given activity holds our deepest attention.

Sacred flow realizes a life in which we learn to live,
move, and simply *be* absorbed in the rhythm and flow of God's
Spirit. Putting rhythm and flow together in light of everyday

Christian spirituality, rhythm describes our life's general everyday movement, while flow occurs when we dive into life's more challenging activities or circumstances. We experience rhythm with God when we attune to his love while engaging in commonplace activities like lazy strolls, hanging out with family, eating dinner, texting a friend, brushing our teeth, checking email, walking the dog, vegging out, driving to work, sleeping, playing with our kids, etc. We find genuine enjoyment in these activities when we give them our full attention, rather than treating them like mundane activities or menacing duties. They seamlessly become part of our rhythm with God.

Flow is movement in the midst of more intense activity or challenge like busy days at the office, intense days at play, demanding service projects, challenging hobbies, fitness training, competing in a competition, deep conversation, etc. In sacred flow, ebb and flow becomes rhythm and flow as we, cognizant of God's love, engage in less demanding and more demanding activities, dive in and pull back, speed up and slow down. Renowned psychologist Abraham Maslow refers to these two experiences as plateau-experiences and peak-experiences.[6] Both are high ground; one wide, flat, and stable, the other narrow, steep, and exhilarating. God's rhythm and flow have us experience high plains and summits even when we walk through valleys of death.

God is a river of rhythm and flow in which we reside. In areas, the river flows gently, sometimes moving so slowly that movement is barely perceptible – rhythm. In other areas, the river races, the water rushes us over rocks creating rapids, quickly and effortlessly dipping and diving – flow. In the sacred flow, we wholly give ourselves to the river's current whatever its pace. We move at varying paces and under continually changing circumstances. We are streams or micro-currents within the river of God. We are one with God, united, always rhythmically flowing in and through him.

losing our religion

In order flow freely in the divine current we've got to lose our religion. Before I encourage you to release your religion, it's necessary for me to more fully define what I mean by religion. I have come to experience religion as any system of beliefs and behaviors (personal or institutional) that when adhered to mean to gain us favor and blessing with God. In other words, only *right* beliefs coupled with *right* behaviors bring spiritual rightness and blessing.

> Let your religion be less of a theory and more of a love affair.
>
> *G.K. Chesterton*

Religion assumes an ongoing separation between God and us. The existence of this gap continues beyond any conversion experience(s) or repeated repentance, and the closure of the gap depends upon acquiring a particular system of beliefs and performing or not performing particular behaviors. The emphasis here lands on the words *system* and *behavior.* Religion is humanity's instituted behavior-oriented pursuit of God. Religion worships order and appropriate behavior. Ironically, religious people are not renowned for their order, unity, and appropriate behavior.

The term religion has several origins. One is the word *religio,* meaning "respect for what is sacred," or "reverence for the gods." But the primary and most popular origin is the Latin *religare* "to bind fast" or "place an obligation on," or a "bond between humans and gods."[7] Fundamentally, religion is meant to bind, bond, or obligate us to God. I would readily admit that my experience with religion has been obligatory and binding.

Reverence, respect, or devotion to God doesn't bother me in the least. Fear or reverence of God is the beginning of wisdom, faith…and sacred flow.[8] Reverence or respect for God provides proper perspective and guides us into his flow. God's wisdom has us acknowledge God's ultimate sovereignty, his constant activity on our behalf, and his intimate union with us. Reverence inspires a deep humility and trust that sets us on a path that diverges from religion toward rhythm. Sacred flow offers reverence without religion.

Being intimately connected or bonded with God sounds great. But I take issue with religion's related premise and practice (more often than not) being human-centered rather than God-centered. It leans too much on the natural rather than supernatural. As *religious* people, we obligate and bind ourselves to God by doing everything possible to please God within our own strength, taking on the role of initiator and responder.

Unwittingly, we reverence God to gain blessing and avoid cursing rather than as a natural rhythm integral to a fulfilled life.

Today many religious leaders perpetuate a lifeless religious system that doesn't work for them personally. They don't recognize the extent of their own crippling religiosity. I didn't. Paradoxically, many stagnant non-flowing religious leaders attempt to teach others how to live in God's sacred flow.

Abraham Maslow wrote about religion, its leaders, and flow. He referred to flow as peak-experience and considered it the pinnacle of human development and experience. He writes the following regarding religious leaders and flow,

> In a word, organized religion can be thought of as an effort to communicate peak-experiences to non-peakers, to teach them, to apply them, etc. Often, to make it more difficult, this job falls into the hands of non-peakers. On the whole we now would expect that this would be a vain effort, at least so far as much of mankind is concerned.[9]

Agreeing with Maslow, I have perceived many religious communities as places where all too often the blind are leading the blind, the stuck are attempting to unstick those who are stuck. Religion inspires fear, panic, frustration, insecurity, and hopelessness. As a religious Christian I experienced all of these negative feelings with varying regularity and intensity. Unfortunately for me and countless others, these feelings (not love) have dominated our relationship with God. It doesn't have to be this way.

Like Maslow, flow's most recognized researcher Hungarian psychologist Mihaly Csikszentmihalyi [Chick-sent-me-high-ee] came to a similar conclusion regarding religion. Dr. Csikszentmihalyi determined that flow, rather than religion, inspires deep focus, meaning, and joy. He doesn't hold out much hope Christianity's future because religion doesn't foster flow. Quite the opposite, he believes the Christian religion leads to spiritual stagnancy rather than flow. Dogmatism and archaic legalistic doctrines corrupt a potentially flowing faith. Given an alternate interpretation and framing, Christianity could be characterized by freedom, constant discovery, focus, and meaningful challenges.[10]

Hope can be found in a faith that flows.

Sacred flow puts us on the path of awareness, focus, purpose, and ultimately joy. Integrated with Christianity, flow's roots and fruits inform and inspire a faith of full engagement and graceful rhythm. Csikszentmihalyi argues that a flowing faith would be a more holistic faith that welcomes and integrates what we know, feel, hope for, and even dread. It would contain a matrix of beliefs that call for, hone, and sustain our attention (devotion) toward meaningful goals (love) thereby providing constant opportunity for flow.[11] Csikszentmihalyi is describing a religion-less Christian faith.

> **Dogmas and creeds and the closed revelation of a completed canon have replaced the emphasis upon keeping close to the fresh uprisings of the Inner Life.**
> *Thomas Kelly*

When Jesus entered the ministry scene, people were being beat up by religion and culture much like I was and you may be right now. The Sisyphus syndrome plagued many people. Fortunately, Jesus came then and comes now offering rest, rhythm, and flow.

> *Are you tired? Worn out? Burned out on religion? Come to me. Get away with me and you'll recover your life. I'll show you how to take a real rest. Walk with me and work with me – watch how I do it. Learn the unforced rhythms of grace. I won't lay anything heavy or ill-fitting on you. Keep company with me and you'll learn to live freely and lightly.*
> *Matthew 11: 28-30, The Message*

The way Eugene Peterson expresses Matthew 11: 28-30 in *The Message* really nourishes me...like a massive plateful of my mom's homemade gnocchi and meatballs bathed in marinara sauce. It's so tasty, organic, meaty, filling, and even light (relatively, I'm Italian). He uses delicious words like "unforced, rhythm, freely, lightly, real, rest, recover, walk, life, grace, watch, and learn."

In these verses Jesus imperatively commands those of us who are heavy burdened with religion, circumstances, or life in general to come to him for rest – an intermission, recreation...a

soul vacation.[12] He promises another way, a rhythmic way. In
other translations of these verses, Jesus encourages his listeners
to take his yoke – *take my yoke upon you and learn from me*. In
Jewish culture, the yoke figuratively represented a rabbi's
interpretation of the Scriptures, specifically the Mosaic Law.
Broader than this, the teacher's yoke was his way of life. Jesus
invites us to follow his lifestyle, his rule, his way, his flow. When
Jesus claims his yoke is easy, the word *easy* can also be translated
comfortable or *better*.[13] His way fits us well, comfortably…best.
Jesus' yoke is not easy for us because he holds a lax view of the
Law or Scriptures, but because taking on Jesus' yoke means he
bears the load for us, in us, and through us. He himself is the
new way, the new flow.

We need this new flow. We must re/turn to God's flow.
We need to reorient our life so that it continuously cultivates the
opportunity for us to experience God's flow. This will require us
to stop our rock-pushing religion and start moving to the grace-
filled rhythm of God.

During the course of their research Csikszentmihalyi
and Maslow did find pockets of Christians experiencing flow.
They discovered flow on the margins with mystics and those
historically declared saints. These people made keeping in step
with God's Spirit a way of life. They experienced God and
served others intensively. They meditated, contemplated, and
served God with extreme awareness, focus, and engagement.
Their source was the indwelling presence of God. They lived in
the sacred flow.

These mystics on the margins serve as our mentors and
models as we move toward a faith that flows. To follow their
lead we must re-center the mystery and mysticism found at the
heart of Christianity.

You might ask, "What mysticism?"
Christ lives in us and we live in him.

This *mutual indwelling* is core to Christianity and the
cornerstone of Christian mysticism. It's the taproot for a flowing
Christianity. It's both fully mysterious and mystical that we have
been placed into God, and he has been placed into us. We
indwell the Flowmaker and he us.

We are meant to flow forth from God and him from us. This sacred flow means to consume our lifestyle, becoming our way of being and doing. It's certainly not meant for the margins. If "Christ in you" is not the center of your faith then what is?

With Christ, the life-giving Spirit, at our center as our source, sacred flow is inherently, dynamically, and mystically Christian. Jesus serves as the initiator, mediator, energy, and sustainer of a flowing faith.

> **The Christian of the future will be a mystic or he will not exist at all.**
> *Karl Rahner*

God saturates our inner core and outer crustiness. He is present in our faith's broadness and minutiae. "Christian" living means that we live according to the promptings and power of the *in*dwelling and *out*dwelling Spirit of God rather than being manipulated by the Sisyphus system, random human inclinations, our spiritual enemy, or surrounding culture.

***

Religion can't save us. It can't provide the meaning or the energy we desire for a fulfilled life – never has, never will. Even worse, "try harder" religion has perverted Christianity, threatening its future. The future requires a faith that flows. Fortunately for us, authentic Christianity flows. Christian spirituality's true mantra is "trust" rather than "try." Trust flows.

Stop your rock-pushing, get off that treadmill. You are free to dive into the current of a God who is trustworthy to float you and flow you. You're meant to float and flow, despite your circumstances. Jesus spoke of a flowing faith when he said, *"Whoever believes in me, as the Scripture has said, streams of living water will flow from within him."*[14] To embrace this living stream spirituality we must lose our religion and find flow – sacred flow.

being formed by God's flow

1. Think through your faith story. How has it been influenced by religion?

2. Take some time to reflect over the terms *rhythm* and *flow*. If needed, invite God to redefine these terms in your context. How does God want to use these ideals to set you free in his flow?

3. How does your faith make room for supernatural mystery and mysticism? Invite God to dissolve any discomfort you have with either and lead you into a healthy engagement of both.

2

Dive into the Flow

The name of the game is to set the busy-ness
of the mind aside and fully bring one's attention
to bear on the immediate task at hand.
Andrew Cooper

I sat in the center of my junior high gymnasium, palms sweating. The thought of walking in front of everyone in the school to receive an award overwhelmed me. I wasn't expected to speak, only walk over, pick up the certificate, walk back, and sit down. *Please God, don't let me trip.* Thankfully, I didn't, but this inconsequential public appearance was only the first of many to come.

My mom used to tell me that someday I would become a public speaker. I have no idea why she said that. Given my shyness it was laughable, and even her comment stressed me out. During high school I was occasionally forced to give presentations, but I never became comfortable with it. College wasn't much different. Through seminary I wasn't up for the challenge, but speaking publicly became a necessary evil.

Eventually, I began helping with a new church that required me to speak at least once a month to a larger group and once a week to a smaller group. I spoke frequently but not with great ease or eloquence. But over time, my goal morphed from simply eluding embarrassment to mastering the material. I wanted to be inspiring and perfect. Unfortunately, no matter how well I did, it wasn't good enough. I spoke with more ease, but it still wasn't enjoyable.

Not until I discovered life in God's flow did I begin to truly enjoy public speaking. I discovered that I could trust in

God rather than solely in my abilities or lack there of. I still prepared well and desired to nail the material but my approach changed. I was no longer distracted by my obsession with perfection. I could prepare, focus, and release myself to speak. It didn't serve me to be pretentious, polished, or perfect. It served me (and everyone else) to simply be me, fully focused and unleashed. I began learning what it means to trust God and release myself into the moment. I discovered flow while speaking and as a result I began having fun. Now I speak quite often and I enjoy it. Mom was right.

> **The truly spiritual man is he that sees God in all things all things in God.**
>
> *William Law*

It's likely that you've released yourself into an activity and were so immersed that all else faded. You've experienced times of seamless connection between your spirit, soul, body, and whatever you are doing. You've sensed time slowing or speeding up as you float along. You've given your undivided attention to something and have been amazed by your seemingly limitless reserve of energy. You've enjoyed the wonder of flow. Flow is a highlight of human experience worthy of discovery and pursuit.

Our desire to flow raises some legitimate questions. Can we set ourselves up to flow? If so, how? What results from our flow? And how exactly does it integrate with our faith? To answer these essential questions will require a more in depth consideration of flow's content and consequences. Csikszentmihalyi and Maslow supply the data we need to better understand flow. Increased understanding of flow will allow us to better use it as a vehicle to carry our Christian spirituality into more intimacy with God.

Csikszentmihalyi initiated usage of the term *flow* as it best represented the idea his research respondents associated with the experience.[15] His initial subjects were artists. These artists were internally motivated and frequently lost themselves in their work.[16] The process or *flow* of creating was far more important than the finished product or what that product might glean financially. Flow became understood as a harmonious experience or state of mind in which we become totally absorbed in what we are doing.[17] Amazingly, Csikszentmihalyi and Maslow found that men and women alike, vastly diverse in age and culture, reported peak experiences in basically the same way despite their activity.[18] Reading and chess nurture flow. So does playing tennis. For the most part, the flow experience is the same for a Chinese teenager as it is for a fifty-five year old Canadian grandfather. They found flow to be a cross-gender, cross-generation, cross-cultural, and cross-activity occurrence (that didn't crossover into mainstream Christianity).

Ultimately, Maslow and Csikszentmihalyi's research hoped to discover what brings us the most enjoyable, abundant life. Csikszentmihalyi asked, "What leads us to optimal experience in our daily lives?" His research concluded that *flow* is fundamental for happiness, enjoyment, development, and wholeness.[19] Maslow, like Csikszentmihalyi, asked a similar fundamental question and discovered a similar result. He inquired, "How can we encourage free development?"[20] He sought to understand the journey toward wholeness. How do we become completely healthy, or more specifically, our authentic self?[21] Both researchers found flow to be integral to a healthy, whole, enjoyable life. Given this, it's essential that our faith be integrated with flow.

the roots of flow

Flow has roots. The root of anything is its core or essence. Our roots are our origin or home. The root is the essential or fundamental part as in "the root of the matter." Roots serve as the source. They are embedded anchors and stabilizers. To be rooted means to be planted or established.

Whether they are roots of a hardwood tree or family roots, healthy roots are vital for proper growth and ultimately fruit. It's safe to say that plants and humans live from their roots, however healthy or unhealthy they may be. Good roots keep us anchored, standing strong, and fed. Good roots mean good fruits. In the context of our daily lives, our roots are our core values or deep focal points. Without sound roots we lack stability, flow, and fruit. Fruit-bearing starts with healthy roots.

Particular roots lay the groundwork for flow. With healthy roots flow may occur in a broad range of contexts. Csikszentmihalyi's extensive research discovered that specific roots grow into flow. Have you ever noticed what inspired your past flow-like experiences? Do you remember being fully focused and engaged? Can you recall the clarity of your goals? Did the activity challenge your skills? Do you remember being flexible and responsive during the activity? These questions echo the roots of flow.

Flow occurs when we are focused, challenged, and responsive to feedback.[22] These three essential roots serve as flow's framework. They are the groundwork of flow. Without focus, challenge, and responsiveness to feedback there is no flow.

Flow embodies an ironic tension – in order to freely flow the recipe must be right. All the roots must be present. You may sense the paradox. How could flow - such a fluid experience - be grounded, rooted, or have rules? The roots seed our activities, allowing flow to germinate, grow, and bear fruit. We needn't approach them as rules or regulations. That will never do. Flow can't be manufactured as such. To flow, the roots must be freely and fluidly engaged.

My speed-reading hobby exemplifies flow's framework. I love learning, but there is so much information and so little time. Speed-reading has provided a way for me to learn faster. While reading, when I'm fully focused and responsive to the book, I automatically speed up and slow down based upon the density (or challenge) of the book's content. At times I breeze along and other times I re-read portions or jot notes in the margin. Flow happens when focus, challenge, and feedback are in play. When 'reading flow' doesn't occur it's likely because I am distracted, disinterested, or unresponsive. I may be scatter-minded, thinking about managing my finances or finding my car keys. Distraction doesn't allow me to dive into the material. Or maybe I'm not distracted but I'm reading something that doesn't interest or challenge me enough, so holding focus proves difficult. Either way, I'm not responsive to feedback from the book, and therefore my reading doesn't flow. Focus, challenge, and feedback prove vital for flow in any context.

focus

In today's frenzied boisterous culture intense concentration is a lost art. Regrettably, we rarely deeply focus. Nevertheless, concentration is the key component of flow. Concentration unifies our consciousness enabling us to disregard things unnecessary for the activity at hand. Without complete attention, flow can't occur. Flow *is* focus.

Concentration's initiation and maintenance largely has to do with our ability to disregard or manage distractions. Too often, we attempt to concentrate in the worst environments; for example, when I try to read in a restaurant play area while my kids are playing. Also, if we're clear about what we're doing--- the goal of our focus---it becomes easier to concentrate deeply. By removing distractions or disregarding them altogether and setting our mind on our activity, concentration more readily begins, deepens, and flow follows.

Timothy Gallwey, the writer of the best selling *Inner Game* books, adds that healthy focus is nonjudgmental. Pure focus rejects condemnation. In order to move our concen-tration toward flow, our self-evaluation mustn't turn to self-deprecation. When we are overly self-conscious or berate ourselves, our vision clouds and concentration breaks (or never truly begins). Non-judgmental awareness as Gallwey calls it, staves off negative distraction allowing concentration to deepen.[23] This brand of observation affords us vision without defensiveness, denial, shame, guilt, or self-doubt.

As someone who has too often tanked mentally, nonjudgmental awareness was a revelation. Spiritually and otherwise, I have suffered often from self-induced paralysis by analysis…or panic. Many of us can easily get locked into overanalyzing practically any circumstance or ourselves. At other times, events occur and we're tempted to freak out rather than back up and take an honest, less emotional look at what has happened. When we overanalyze or panic, we become anxious and angry rather than cool, calm, and focused. Nonjudgmental awareness offers us a way to candidly evaluate our situations and invite God's wisdom without losing our rhythm.

> **God has given to the earth the breath which feeds it. It is his breath that gives life to all things. And if he were to hold his breath, everything would be annihilated. His breath vibrates in yours, in your voice. It is the breath of God that you breathe – and you are unaware of it.**
> *Theophilus of Antioch*

25

In addition to being non-judgmental, flow-like focus remains in the moment and specifically on the activity. The goal is the activity. Csikszentmihalyi initially considered this idea a psychological anomaly. Why would anyone do something so attentively, so passionately, without external motivation or expectation of reward? Eventually, he termed this anomaly *autotelic*, derived from two Greek roots: *auto* meaning self and *telos* meaning goal. The goal is the activity itself.[24] Autotelically, we engage in any given activity for the sake of participation in the activity. Enjoyment relates to our participation in the activity, not merely reward. Csikszentmihalyi believes this approach can become our way of life. We can dedicate our complete attention and intention to each moment creating a lifestyle that flows.

Living this attentively in a culture that cherishes multi-tasking and results proves to be a daunting challenge. We easily default to acting for results and reward. In children we see hope for responding differently. We regularly see the *autotelic* approach with kids at play. They regularly become absorbed in their activities. While building a ten-foot tall teepee in our front yard from scrap tree branches my kids are not distracted by 95 degree heat, hunger, or the near future hassle of dismantling it before the neighbors freak out. They are totally tuned in to teepee building; placing a branch, evaluating, finding the next branch, placing that branch, and so on.

> **For God's love is like a river springing up in the depth of the Divine Substance and flowing endlessly through His creation, filling all things with life and goodness and strength.**
> **Thomas Merton**

challenge

Have you every wondered what drives us to test our mental or physical limits? Why do we willingly attempt feats that tax our capabilities? Something instinctual motivates us to push ourselves. Oddly, we enjoy challenge…maybe because it leads to flow.

Challenge is a must for flow. We typically initiate self-induced challenges by goal-setting. As a grace lover, something about setting goals feels unnatural. I'm no slacker, it's just that goal-setting often feels legalistic, rigid, or as if I'm following the steps in an infomercial success kit. Nevertheless, I know goals don't have to sour my soul. It's really about why I am setting them, their content, how I set them, hold them, move toward them, and relate to them. It's my personal culture of goals that needs tending. You, too, may need a cultural correction regarding goals.

Goals provide forward movement for our focus. Clarity of our intention helps us focus our attention and deal with distractions. If our goals are vague or unreachable, focus falters and flow never begins. To some extent, goals make our desires measurable and therefore more pursuable.

Goals are necessary but not meant to be pursued mechanically. While flowing, we pursue goals with rhythmic natural action, not emotionless precision or disjointed clumsiness. Our daily "to do" list at home or the office can become a set of goals that we approach rhythmically. These can be understood as desires for the day, goals creating opportunities for flow. I took this approach at a corporate job I had a few years ago. My morning rhythm started by establishing my goals for the day. Once I settled in, I poured myself into these tasks one by one. When I did this my days sped by, I enjoyed them more, and I got plenty of work done.

Those of us in creative roles or undertaking more subjective activities (like walking in step with God's Spirit) may experience considerable tension when faced with goal-setting. Csikszentmihalyi acknowledges the difficulty artists and others who work in the abstract face in setting clear goals. He stresses their need to form some kind of unconscious internal means to inform their direction and decisions.[25] They need to set goals, but must do so intuitively.

What about the many days we go about life with weak or nonexistent motivation and goals? Inevitably, life forces us to do things we don't particularly desire or have a low level of skills to accomplish, i.e. some items on my daily "to do" list mentioned above. This is just the reality of life. Csikszentmihalyi discovered what he termed *emergent* motivation and goals. If full engagement in these humdrum activities continues, our focus may generate motivation, goal-setting, and eventually flow.[26] Emergent motivation makes flow possible in some of life's most unexpected or mundane activities.

Regardless of our motivation, for flow to occur with any predictability a delicate balance must be struck between the challenge we face and our skill level. To experience flow, our skill level must match the demand at hand. Csikszentmihalyi calls this equilibrium the *challenge-skills balance* (CS balance), the "golden rule" of flow.[27] Have you ever noticed how much more fun you have when you play any game with someone of equal ability rather than someone much better or much worse? If our skills grossly overwhelm theirs we become bored. If their skills substantially trump ours, then anxiety or frustration distracts or consumes us. I prove this true every time I play tennis. If I play with my friend John, with whom I am equally terrible, we often flow and thoroughly enjoy the experience. However, if I play my friend Jo, he gets bored quickly and I get embarrassed. Flow begins at low skill levels in any given activity as long as our challenge matches our skill level. As our skills grow we must engage in more difficult challenges in order to experience flow.

> Ah! dear friend, you little know the possibilities which are in you.
> *Charles H. Spurgeon*

Flow also relates to life's ultimate goal and meaning. Csikszentmihalyi asserts that we make life meaningful when an ultimate goal or purpose extends our influence beyond ourselves and guides our choice of secondary goals.[28] We thrive when our life has meaning and a goal beyond ourselves. We manage life's stressors better when we consider challenges (obstacles) as opportunities for flow experiences along the way to accomplishing our ultimate goals. Our inner conflict recedes when meaningful goals are settled and given full attention.[29] In other words, inner peace comes when we know what we want, what we want is meaningful, and we pour ourselves into it. This big picture goal-setting makes way for a lifestyle of flow.

feedback

In order to nurture flow we need feedback. Our source of feedback may be internal, external, or both. While competing, successful athletes acutely tune in to their body, evaluate the feedback, and make adjustments.[30] In addition to our intuition, most of us have someone (or too many) around us offering feedback. Unfortunately, many of us deny or neglect useful feedback, fail to adjust, and therefore miss opportunities to experience flow. When we have a good sense of how the activity is going, tweaking may occur to initiate or maintain our flow.

For artists and the like, Csikszentmihalyi once more confesses the existence of a tension, as with goals. Who gives writers or sculptors real-time feedback? Here again, those involved in creative or subjective activity must rely primarily on intuitive feedback. They must know where their work is going, when it is on or off track, and when it is finished. Csikszentmihalyi calls this, "internalizing the rules and the judgments of the field."[31] They know (or learn) their domain well enough to know what is great, what's not, and what needs to be done going forward. They intuitively discern and respond.

This reminds me of when I saw Vincent Van Gogh's *Starry Night* painting at the High Museum of Art in Atlanta. Two things were particularly striking; its beauty and texture. Without a doubt I can say it's a masterful, moving piece of art. It has incredible flow. Noticeably, some places on the canvas were rich with color and depth, yet in other places bare canvas peeked through. It's so clumpy in some places and bare in others that some observers might consider it unfinished. Van Gogh didn't think so.

Summarizing the roots that inspire flow, Csikszentmihalyi says, "It matters little what you do, what matters is how you do it."[32] But this is no secret to us, really. We lived this way as kids and our parents or grandparents have told us this plenty of times. We just didn't know it was backed by decades of research. Challenge yourself, fully focus on whatever it is you are doing, and be responsive to feedback.

the fruits of flow

Maslow and Csikszentmihalyi both discovered a number of universal characteristics that serve as both distinctive markers and fruits of the flow experience – *what you feel when you flow*. You'll likely recognize these more than the roots that set the stage for flow. These distinctive effects of flow compel us to return to flow as often as possible. Rightfully so, they are flavorful fruits.

Synthesizing the research of Maslow, Csikszentmihalyi, and others, the following characteristic fruits mark flow: a sense of unity, validation, identity, absorption, inner peace, effortlessness, control, selflessness, timelessness, and emotional balance.[33] Encapsulating many of these effects, basketball great Bill Russell described his experience by reporting feelings "of profound joy, an acute intuition, a feeling of effortlessness in the midst of intense exertion, a sense of the action taking place in slow motion, feelings of awe and perfection, increased mastery, and self-transcendence."[34]

Flow has been referred to as a *unitive* experience. In these moments we perceive everything as unified, beautiful, and whole.[35] Flow inexplicably heightens our perception of the interrelation of all things. We catch a glimpse of God-like perspective. We pour ourselves into something and suddenly the world pops, or as my friend Billy says, "It goes 3-D." We see everything in all its dimensions, its fullness, connected.

I remember experiencing '3-D' unity while on a sailboat in Greece with people from eight countries. As the sun sank into the Aegean Sea our boat gently bobbed as we talked about the deeper things in our very different but very similar lives. The unity amidst our diversity became palpable.

Flow is *self-validating*. Maslow called peak-experiences end-experiences rather than means-experiences.[36] They validate or justify themselves. They are an end unto themselves. When a deep flow experience occurs we feel awe, grace, and gratitude so much so that we live to collect more of these experiences. We often feel something special has just happened. Maslow writes, "The peak-experiences of pure delight are for my subjects among the ultimate goals of living and the ultimate validations and justifications for it."[37] The flow experience in and of itself carries significant weight and meaning. Since flow is self-validating, it pays to pay attention. Flow, in and of itself, is a worthy pay off.

Peak-experience strengthens our sense of *identity*. When flowing, it feels like we're functioning within our true self; a real self not experienced or fully perceived when we're not flowing.[38] With regard to this, Maslow goes as far as to say that only peakers can achieve their full identity.[39] While flowing, we come closer to our real selves, reaching or even exceeding our potential. Fully pouring ourselves into the activity at hand allows us to experience and express our true identity.

Attention invested in any moment may increase to the point of total *absorption*. How many times have you been in a great conversation with a friend and eventually looked at your watch to find an inordinate amount of time had passed? The restaurant where you were meeting emptied and the staff was waiting for you to leave. You were totally absorbed in the conversation. This absorption can happen with anything interesting or challenging enough to hold our attention completely.[40] We become totally lost in the moment. Some athletes describe this as a "cocoon of "concentration" or a "player's trance".[41]

Total absorption into our activity leads to a unification of our awareness and action, making us feel at one with our activity. The dualism between our activity and our self fades. You might have said or heard people say things like, "My skis felt like extensions of my feet," "My racket was an extension of my hand," or "I actually felt as if I were a character in the story I was reading."

Our brain chemically aids attention and absorption. When we focus our attention, our brain excretes the neurotransmitter dopamine, fixing our attention and encouraging us to continue. As we give more attention, more dopamine is released.[42] Enough dopamine can make us feel slightly high or 'doped up.' This might explain the physical euphoria sometimes associated with flow and why we sense our awareness and action becoming one. To the contrary, it has been postulated that a link exists between attention deficit hyperactivity disorder (ADHD) and dopamine dysfunction.[43] Without the proper amount of dopamine we struggle to maintain focus.

> **God is a flowing and ebbing sea, which flows without ceasing into all his beloved, according to everyone's need and dignity.**
> *Jan van Ruusbroec*

Inner peace also characterizes flow. This calm gives credence to the general sense of wellbeing or harmony we experience when flowing. Many people testify to experiencing deep peace or inner stillness, calmness within fear, during chaotic circumstances or extreme risk.[44] The body de-stresses when fully tuned. Fear, anxiety, inhibition, irrational restraint, and confusion disappear. We truly relax.

Flow allows us to *effortlessly* operate even while taxing our mental and physical capacities.[45] The whole person functions in concert with unforced rhythm. Though the body may be pushing itself to its limits and beyond, while flowing, it does so gracefully. Peak-performance seems to simply happen. When professional artists or athletes do extraordinary things they do so spontaneously, fluidly without intentional reflection upon prior instruction or practice.[46] Appropriate responses happen naturally and effortlessly with appropriate timing. This grace doesn't negate training; it manifests and transcends it.

While flowing we feel that we have much greater *control* over our environment and ourselves. Mysteriously, we believe we can affect exactly what happens, how it happens, and when it happens. We respond to our circumstances with an inordinate sense of command over ourselves. Additionally, anxiety related to loss of control doesn't distract us while flowing. When experiencing this sensation of increased mastery and supreme control, we feel free to engage new and more extreme challenges.[47]

> **There is rest for everything and movement for everything and these come from that which, transcending rest and movement, establishes each being according to an appropriate principle and gives each the movement suitable to it.**
>
> *Pseudo-Dionysius*

Flow leads to a lack of self-consciousness. In as sense, we become *selfless*. Pretension, doubt, fear, and low self-esteem subside. Undivided focus neutralizes self-interference, negative self-talk, and self-condemnation.[48] We have no attention left to experience anxiety about the way we perceive ourselves, or are perceived by others. Csikszentmihalyi explains this loss of self-consciousness is not a loss of self, or of consciousness, but a loss of consciousness of self.[49] We become more conscious than any other time without being self-focused.

While consumed with the moment, we experience an altered sense of time or *timelessness*. Our sense of time gets warped as hours pass by in what feels like minutes, or minutes stretch out to what seems like hours.[50] We move with lightening-like quickness or seemingly in slow motion. Time integrates into our experience. It mysteriously warps as if it were under our control or even nonexistent. This reflects the old adage, "Time flies when you're having fun."

Experiencing all these fruits, it makes sense that we would be more *emotionally balanced*. While flowing we are emotional, but buoyant, floating, gently bobbing within our circumstances. We're able to embrace emotions without being controlled by them. We process and integrate positive and negative emotions without slipping from flow. We've seen this buoyancy or lack there of in competition many times. One competitor maintains consistent focus and composure coming away victorious while the other competitor falters becoming mentally or emotionally unbalanced.

Many covet the fruits of flow. However, without roots there are no fruits. Giving full attention to the framework of flow whatever we do is a pre-condition for flow. Focus, challenge, and feedback set us up for flow. With this framework established fruits will surely follow.

***

Flow is a phenomenon practically everyone acknowledges but few can sufficiently articulate and pursue. Diving into the flow his chapter helped us better understand flow by closely considering its roots and fruits. Having established and described flow's framework and fruits, we are ready to integrate it with Christian spirituality. To begin, it's only sensible that we start with Jesus. The next chapter shares something revolutionary – Jesus flows.

being formed by God's flow

1. Think about times you have experienced flow. Did you sense God's presence? As you reflect over these experiences ask God to reveal himself within them. Going forward, give attention to God's presence as you experience flow.
2. What are the roots of your daily life? What anchors your rhythm? Give God permission to reset, reframe, or re-prioritize your roots.
3. Invite God to examine the fruits (or lack thereof) you experience in daily life. Do they reflect the fruit of the

Spirit or the fruits of flow? If not, ask God to specifically reveal what is hindering you.

3

Jesus Flows

The Word always flows!
Meister Eckhart

If we're not careful 98% of our life can be lost in some form of hustle and bustle. Our movement becomes a blur without focus or intention, without flow. This seems to creep into every facet of our personal and professional lives. We hustle to get ready in the morning, hurry the kids along to school, hustle to class or work, hustle to start and finish projects, hurry home, hustle to dinner, hurry the kids to bed, and then collapse into bed ourselves. Any restful rhythm we experience throughout our day, spiritual or otherwise, gets sidetracked quite easily.

Has it ever occurred to you that Jesus never hustled, hurried…or bustled? He kept a rhythmic pace. In addition, he always had sufficient ability and energy to carry out what each situation demanded of him. His restful rhythm was well established and maintained. It seems that if anyone should have hurried it's a messiah who had the span of about three years to save humankind. He simply did not hurry, more to the opposite. He told stories and spent a lot of time with friends and sick people. He never pretentiously showed off divine ability or energy. He flowed along rhythmically with care.

Jesus' lack of hustle and bustle and his humble wielding of ability and energy offer us hope. He tuned in to another paradigm regarding his perception of time, energy, and activity. He moved with grace and peace guided by his Father. Jesus flowed. As Jesus' followers, friends, brothers and sisters, co-heirs, and carriers of his Spirit, our birthright is to live as he did.

Jesus is the flow

Paradise was lost when our original ancestors surrendered their divine Source. They were given more than adequate supply in a glorious, lush garden. They flowed in relationship with God their provider. The Tempter then offered the undeniable - self-sourcing - something beyond intended human capacity. They had an opportunity to be like God, determining good and evil, right and wrong, a capacity difficult to refuse. Conversely, they were meant to freely flow in the life of God, allowing him to make value judgments and determine direction. Their independence would secure creative control of their lives...or at least the illusion of it. They would become their own creators and life-givers. In striking out on their own, they lost their Source. They lost touch with the *Logos*; God's life, wisdom, creative energy, and revelation.

> *In the beginning was the Word [Logos], and the Word was with God, and the Word was God. He was in the beginning with God. All things came into being through Him, and apart from Him nothing came into being that has come into being. In Him was life, and the life was the light of men. The light shines in the darkness, and the darkness did not comprehend it...And the Word became flesh, and dwelt among us, and we saw His glory, glory as the only begotten from the Father, full of grace and truth.*
> John 1: 1-5, 14

The *Logos* is the flow that is both of God and from God. The *Logos* serves as God's agent implementing his will. Writer George Maloney affirms this, writing, "All things are created through the Logos, through whom the creative will of the Father flows."[51] Christian culturist Leonard Sweet adds, "Every religion has a 'root metaphor' that gives it depth and substance...For the Christian it is the *Logos*."[52] Jesus serves as both the substance and the agent of the *Logos* – God's creative flow.

Historically, the Greek term *logos* has carried several meanings. The English term *word* only hints at its capacity. In Greek philosophy *logos* was understood as the coherent universal cosmic principle of order and reason, the unifying force of the universe.[53] The *logos was* to thank for humankind's rational capacity.

In Jewish thought, the *Logos* referred to God in action, particularly in creation, revelation, and redemption.[54] They also understood it as personified wisdom, the thought of God. The *Logos* is the self-expression of God; more than a single word; it is the whole message that reveals God.[55]

In the Gospel of John we read that the *Logos* served as the agent of creation and later was incarnate in creation.[56] Integrating these ideas we could say the *Logos* is the divine Intent, the ultimate Wisdom, the Reality, the divine Cause, the Source, the Almighty Breath, the creative Energy, and the eternal Agent of God.

The New Testament adds another profound dimension – the *Logos* is a person, Jesus. He is personable and personal. The *Logos* is intimate, inviting, and compassionate. Jesus is the culmination of the integration of all things *logos*. All things emanate from him, are for him, and return to him.[57]

Jesus *is* energy. Sweet agrees declaring the *Logos* as an "energy releasing event and essential for the emergence of life, biological or spiritual."[58] This relates to the *Logos* as the Source and the Cause. Also, John describes the *Logos* as both the life and the light. He writes, "In Him was life, and the life was the light of men."[59] This *Logos*-life light became

> The divine Logos, who once for all was born in the flesh, always in His compassion desires to be born in spirit in those who desire Him.
> *Maximus the Confessor*

human. He is the divine current, flowing from God lighting up all of creation including its primary creatures - us. Integrating many of the metaphoric identities assigned to Jesus into the term *Logos* English mystic Evelyn Underhill writes,

> The Logos, which is in essence the energetic expression of the Divine Nature, creative Spirit ever seeking to penetrate and mould the material world, he describes as Light struggling with darkness, as the "Life of men," pouring itself out from the fountain of Godhead like "living water"; as the Bread which feeds man, the Paraclete which perpetually helps and enlightens him, the Door through which finite returns to infinite; the

37

living, growing Vine of which men are but the branches; and at the same time as the personal Son of God, the Saviour and Shepherd of Souls. This richly-various manifestation of Eternal Reality, he says, broke out through mankind in its perfect and "saving" form in the person of Jesus of Nazareth. There the divine energy found its perfect thoroughfare, and appeared "in the flesh."[60]

Logos-light flowed into the world as Jesus. John writes that Jesus is the Light that enlightens everyone. Jesus comes offering God's life, revelation, discovery, and awakening – light. His flow illuminates everything in its path, unmatched by the darkness that comes against it. God-light brings God's reality.

Jesus embodies Trinitarian energy flow. Theologian Miroslav Volf states that in Jesus' incarnation the interflow of the Trinitarian energy became "outbound flow" into humanity.[61] Jesus represents divine life in human form and offers us his form of life.[62] Jesus is the full flow of God made human, both as the possessor and giver of God's life.[63] As a person of the Trinity, Jesus has and will always flow. He enjoys perfect union with the Father and the Holy Spirit. The three persons of the Trinity, being distinct identities, participate in and with one another to the extent that all is united, shared, and mutually exchanged.[64] Jesus flows forth from the Trinity as the *Logos* exposing and expressing God and grants us access to the Trinity.[65]

> **Character in a saint means the disposition of Jesus persistently manifested.**
> *Oswald Chambers*

God invites us to fully receive his divine current, to regain the Source. Astonishingly, we're meant to house Jesus, the *Logos*-flow, within us. In a mysterious but real sense, we have joined the interflow of the Trinity.[66] The flow dwells richly within us and we dwell in him.

Jesus flows

In addition to the profundity of Jesus *being* flow, Jesus, in his humanity, modeled flow as a way of life. In doing so, he demonstrated authentic humanness, the way God intended us to live. He spent his time doing a myriad of natural (and supernatural) activities moving rhythmically within the confines of a mostly typical human life for his era. He walked a lot, worked a lot; he ate, slept, celebrated, mourned, and worshiped. He spoke publicly and spent plenty of time with friends. Also, Jesus regularly pulled away to be alone with the Father. His un-rushed rhythm modeled to us a healthy way of life. He did everything in tune with and empowered by his Father. Jesus flowed.

> *For the one whom God has sent speaks the words of God,*
> *for God gives the Spirit without limit. The Father loves*
> *the Son and has placed everything in his hands.*
> *John 3: 34-35*

Considering Jesus' life alongside flow's roots we see the manner and depth of his flow. Sticking to the roots of flow, we find plenty of focus, challenge and feedback in Jesus' life. He *focused* upon the Father and his will. He was fully present for people and tasks. Jesus was *challenged* or tested in various ways throughout his earthly life. In his relationship with the Father, he enjoyed constant conversation and *feedback*.

Jesus' flow was rooted in his union with God. We needn't read very much of the New Testament to glean that Jesus lived in perfect union with his Father. John's gospel records many of Jesus' sayings related to union or mutual indwelling with the Father. He not only claimed that God sent him but that he and God were one. Jesus reported that he was *in* the Father and the Father was *in* him. He declared that if you have seen him you have seen the Father. Jesus boldly claimed to possess the glory of God.[67]

Jesus understood himself to be absorbed in the Father and simultaneously dependent. He surrendered his divine privileges, choosing to operate in dependent unison with his Father God. He was given the mission and privilege of flowing forth from his Father every moment of his earthly existence. His flow took the form of a fully awakened and attuned human.

> *Therefore Jesus answered and was saying to them,*
> *'Truly, truly, I say to you, the Son can do nothing of Himself,*
> *unless it is something He sees the Father doing; for whatever the*

Father does, these things the Son also does in like manner.
John 5: 19

Many texts, in the gospel of John particularly, support the idea of Jesus flowing. The verse above doesn't communicate subordination but unity or harmony of action. The son followed in his Father's footsteps like an exceptional apprentice.[68] Jesus, deeply concentrating upon the Father, chose to do whatever the Father initiated, approved, or did himself. They operated in perfect concert with one another.

I can do nothing on My own. I judge as God
tells me. Therefore, my judgment is just, because I
carry out the will of the one who sent me, not my own will.
John 5: 30

As the living Father sent Me, and I live because of the Father,
so he who eats of Me, he also will live because of Me.
John 6: 57

Jesus stressed his complete abandonment to the initiation and authority of the Father on several occasions. He actually said that he did *nothing* without the Father. What he did, he did in connection with and empowered by the Father. His life came directly from the Father. He was the prophet-son, a conduit meant to send a message exactly as the message sender required.[69] Jesus' whole life flowed. Jesus repeatedly claims that he has come to do the will of his Father, not his own.

Those who have the wind of the Holy Spirit in their souls glide ahead even while they sleep.
Brother Lawrence

For I have come down from heaven, not to do My
own will, but the will of Him who sent Me.
John 6: 38

Do you not believe that I am in the Father, and the Father is in Me?
The words that I say to you I do not speak on My own initiative, but
the Father abiding in Me does His works.
John 14: 10

The will of God served as Jesus' singular focus. Jesus didn't claim that he did any work "for God." Instead, he said the Father dwelling in him did works through him. He claimed the works he did were actually God's. God's work flowed through him.

> *So Jesus answered them and said, "My teaching*
> *is not Mine, but His who sent Me."*
> *John 7: 16*

> *For I did not speak on My own initiative, but the Father*
> *Himself who sent Me has given Me a commandment*
> *as to what to say and what to speak. I know that His*
> *commandment is eternal life; therefore the things I*
> *speak, I speak just as the Father has told Me.*
> *John 12: 49-50*

Jesus' teaching and spoken words were given to him by the Father. Jesus gave perfect and complete expression to God.[70] The Father even shared with him *how* to say what he said. Jesus flowed so closely with the Father that he understood the tone with which the Father would have him speak. This constituted an incomprehensible level of intimacy. The Father acted in and through the person of Jesus…still does. The Father mediates his life to all of humankind through the Spirit of Jesus.[71]

Jesus' life and ministry aligned naturally and seamlessly with the roots of flow.

> *Focus* – upon the Father and those in his presence.
> *Challenge* – carry out the will of the Father.
> *Feedback* – respond to the Father and Holy Spirit.

He *focused* upon the Father. He lived attentively, intrinsically motivated and in complete harmony with the Father. He lived each moment mindfully. His *challenge* was to trust his Father throughout his life, suffering, and death. His definitive goal was the Father's will. His *feedback* came from the other two persons of the Trinity. His mind, body, and movement were one with God.

These roots are evident in many stories in the life of Jesus. They manifested themselves organically. One primary example is Jesus' encounter with the Samaritan woman at the well in Sychar. Jesus, tired from his long walk from Judea into Galilee, sat down at a well. A Samaritan woman came along to pull up some water. Jesus acknowledged the woman and asked a favor – *Give me a drink*. He offered his full attention in a discussion that radically changed her life. This was totally adverse to the culture and the woman was readily aware of it. Shocked, she responded, "How is it that you, a Jew, ask me for a drink since I am Samaritan woman?" Being fully engaged, he betrayed the cultural standards of ignoring her as both Samaritan and a woman.

In tune with the Father and in conversation with the woman, Jesus divulged his identity and mission. He declared himself the living flow, the Messiah, for whom she and everyone else was waiting. With feedback from the Father, he exposed her wayward lifestyle and offered himself as life. This simple encounter with the Christ, God's flow, brought her into alignment with the Father. He drew this outcast into his flow – transforming her understanding of God and self

> **In him he has expressed everything he can do and, most of all, what he wishes to do. Thus all things have been expressed in him, his Son – in that center, which, so to speak is his art...**
>
> *Bonaventure*

and moving her from resistance to divine romance. Leaving the water pot, she went into the city to tell others of her encounter with the Messiah.

Today, we represent both the Samaritan woman and Jesus. As outcasts ignorant of living water, we meet a God who confronts our thirst-driven waywardness and invites us without condition to drink up God's flow. Then, as those containing the flow and living from it, we courageously move according to a love-rhythm that has us touch the untouchables in our cultural context offering them life-giving flow.

Besides the Gospels providing examples of Jesus living from the roots of flow, they also furnish examples of Jesus exhibiting the fruits of flow. Jesus projected all of flow's fruits: a sense of unity, self-validation, identity, absorption, inner peace, effortlessness, control, selflessness, timelessness, and emotional balance. Granted, we may think flow's fruits seem more fitting for Eastern religions, but in fact they effectively express the way of Jesus. Hopefully any discomfort we have with them will fade after considering them in the context of Jesus' life and our relationship with him.

As the agent of creation and its sustainer, the beginning and the end, Jesus consciously understood all things as connected, interrelated, and *unified*. He experienced union with the Father even as he walked the earth. He understood the big picture: how his story would unite history. Conscious of where his life was going, Jesus mentioned his impending suffering and death and its ultimate unifying purpose. Jesus, the sum of all things, flowed in concert with the Father's plan and the unity of all things.

> *He is before all things and in him all things hold together.*
> *Colossians 1: 17*

Jesus' flow *validated his identity* and the mission of God. He confessed that his food was to do the will of the Father. His sacred flow with the Father was an end in itself. As noted earlier, many statements in John's gospel reflect that Jesus' validation came in being himself – the son of God. His everyday movement with the Father as the *Logos*, the revelation of God, validated him and those who embraced him. Jesus served as presence and validity for a seemingly unreachable God.

Jesus' unique *identity* was established prior to him doing any official "ministry." As Jesus was baptized, a dove descended upon him and the voice of God confirmed his identity as the beloved Son of God. As he flowed with the Father toward execution, it's clear that he grasped his unique identity. Jesus claimed himself as the *path*, the *route*, the *road*, and the *gate* to the Father. In Luke's gospel when the council of elders presses him about his identity he admitted that he was the son of God and the expected Messiah. While with his friends, Jesus transfigured and God acknowledged again that Jesus was his son in whom he is well pleased. His identity was repeatedly authenticated and expressed through his flow with the Father.

Jesus' whole life was *absorbed* in the Father. Remember, he said that he lived because of the Father. He was in the Father and the Father in him. Jesus was God expressed in humanity. Additionally, Jesus did nothing outside of the intention of the Father. He tuned in to the Father for what to do and when to do it as well as what to say and how to say it. John writes that the Jews marveled at what Jesus knew of the Scriptures without having formally studied. This would be impossible without his attention being absorbed in the Father.

Throughout his life Jesus acted out of an *inner peace* or stillness. Nothing rattled him. He faced down the evil one for forty days in the desert without losing his cool. When he was questioned about a woman accused of adultery just prior to her being stoned, he stooped, wrote in the dirt, and diffused the whole event with a profound invitation – *let he who has no sin cast the first stone.* When his life was in jeopardy by Pharisee-endorsed assassination attempts, he calmly and quietly slipped away. He slept peacefully in an undersized boat during an oversized storm. Awakened by his anxious friends, he calms the storm with a few words. Knowing he faced flogging and execution, he didn't have a meltdown and flee. He wrestled with his role for a moment, but he didn't panic. When Peter hacked off an ear at the moment of Jesus' apprehension, Jesus calmly reattached the ear and turned himself in to the guards. He was fully attuned to the Father and his ultimate goal – offering new life and union to everyone who would receive it.

Jesus worked *effortlessly* in the power of the Father. He carried out miraculous feats without strain. He fed over five thousand with barely enough food for three. He turned vats of water into fine wine. He healed countless people without hesitation or stress; including those in need of resurrection or the casting out of demons. This is not to say that his ministry was not demanding. But in the midst of the demands he moved with unforced rhythm. He did not cave in to the huge expectations placed upon him. He glided. Even in the garden, in his toughest hour, he processed his fear and pain and moved forward in the will of his Father.

Jesus' projected *control* often by wielding authority over the spiritual and physical realms. As already mentioned, he fed crowds, calmed the storm, turned water into wine, healed the sick, cast out demons, walked on water, and even raised the dead. He ran the money changers out of the Temple as if he owned the place. He knew what others were thinking. Perhaps most powerfully, he knew his life was under the control of the Father. His control projected the Father's. Tuned in to the Father's voice and timing, he was in touch with his story and destiny. Ultimately, Jesus' control led him to an excruciating death, ordinary burial, and a supernatural resurrection in order to usher in a new way of life all of humanity.

Ironically, Jesus' sense of control allowed him to move spontaneously. He didn't have a set schedule. He moved guided by the Father. This movement cost his good friend Lazarus his life and led to his resurrection. Jesus, knowing of Lazarus' sickness, stalled instead of picking up his pace. He arrived four days after Lazarus' demise to find a very dead, stinking corpse. He later explained that his stalling had to do with the Father's guidance and glory. In another story, Jesus went to a dinner party on a whim with a little man of ill repute.

> Hasten to the springs, draw from the wells. In God is the wellspring of life, a spring that can never fail. In his light is found a light that nothing can darken. Desire that light which your eyes know not! Your inward eye is preparing to see the light. You inward thirst burns to be quenched at the spring.
>
> *Augustine*

Remember Zacchaeus? Jesus was walking through Jericho when he spots Zacchaeus up in a tree. Jesus invites himself over to Zacchaeus' house for dinner.[72] The Spirit-wind blew him about in a God-intentioned pattern.

Jesus was *selfless*. Selfishness or self-consciousness didn't factor into his way of life. He focused upon the Father rather than himself – *not my will but yours be done*. He didn't have high or low self esteem; he had appropriate self-esteem. He gracefully valued himself and others. He had nothing to prove. He was secure in his identity as a beloved Son of God. John's account of the last supper provides an example of Jesus' *other-*consciousness. After supper, Jesus washed his friends' feet. This act embodied a selfless disposition. Jesus, with perfect self-esteem and confidence in where he had come from and where he was going, took on the lowliest job of the day in order to serve his friends and set an example.[73] Soon afterward, he allowed himself to be beaten almost to the point of death only to be later executed as a criminal. He endured this shame not being conscious of himself but of us and our need.[74]

Jesus is truly *timeless*. He uniquely experiences time. He exists inside and outside of time as a person of the Trinity. He is the beginning and the end – the Alpha and the Omega, eternal,

and yet present to each one of us in each moment. He is I AM.
He saturates the time-space continuum bending it at the will of
the Father. He altered the course of human history and
humanity's destiny in what was likely less then three years of
public presence. His death and resurrection happened in a few
days, but affect all of time and eternity. Jesus is the eternal life
and offers this timeless life to everyone.[75]

Jesus' life portrayed *emotional balance*. He was never
really high or really low for any significant period of time, but he
fully experienced his emotions. He expressed intense emotions
but didn't allow them to dominate his attitude or actions. He
wept over Jerusalem, when Lazarus died, and he was tormented
to the point of sweating blood at Gethsemane. Most certainly,
the forty-day desert temptation was an emotional experience.

> **Jesus Christ does not want to be our helper. He wants to be our life. He does not want us to work for Him. He wants us to let Him do His work through us.**
> *Charles G. Trumball*

When tempted in the wilderness,
instead of giving in to the
emotional manipulation of his
enemy, he responded with truth
from his Father's words. During
his ministry he was headed for
suffering and death yet he
continued onward with an even
emotional keel. In the garden
during his final moments of
freedom, he was terribly troubled but allowed himself to
continue in the flow of God's will. Despite what he encountered,
Jesus embraced emotion, processed it, and moved forward
without being crippled, paralyzed, or overwhelmed.

prodigal flow

God prodigally flows. Jesus' parable about the lost son
illustrates God's wild flow. Popularly called *The Prodigal Son,*
this story would more aptly be titled *Prodigal Father* or *Prodigal
Love*. The term prodigal means *wastefully* or *recklessly extravagant,
lavishly abundant*. The father's love in this story is *prodigal*. He
gives his ungrateful young son his inheritance prematurely. This
ingrate son goes out and squanders all he has. The father
demonstrates prodigal love when he sees his returning son from
afar. Unthinkably, the father runs to him and kisses him (literally
falls on his neck), a very prodigal thing to do. Then, in an

unprecedented manner, he calls for the best robe in the house, the family signet ring, shoes, and a homecoming party. What an absurd love.

Finally, the father leaves the party to meet his disgruntled *un*compassionate pouting older son whose relationship and inheritance he reassures. Clearly, this father has lost his senses just as his young son returned to his. This story vividly communicates God's prodigal character, particularly his reckless love for people. God wildly flows, intensely and compassionately seeking us, always inviting us home.

If we could really grasp just how prodigal is his flow, I'm afraid many of us would be offended like the older brother. God's flow created the universe and all things in it. God's prodigal presence saturates the earth. Everyone on earth throughout history has benefited from his prodigal flow whether they have acknowledged God or not. He extravagantly flows establishing and sustaining all things. God unremittingly makes this flow available to everyone - even those who refuse to acknowledge his existence or blatantly disrespect him. Gracefully, he lavishes his *Logos*-life and love - perpetually calling people into a deeper experience of his sacred flow. God's flow is unstoppable regardless of our regard or disregard.

***

Maslow, Csikszentmihalyi, Sweet, and other researchers have tapped into a flow phenomenon that has profound, meaningful connection with life of Jesus. Jesus is the prodigal *Logos*-flow given into humanity and into us. Jesus' lifestyle was an archetype. He lived a super and natural life, modeling dependent rhythm and flow with the Father, demonstrating to us the only way to be truly human. The next chapter builds a bridge between Jesus' experience of sacred flow and our faith. Jesus secured for us a level of intimacy with the Father that few of us have ever really experienced or expressed. He provides himself as the substance of our sacred flow leading us into his way of life.

being formed by God's flow

1. Consider what it means for Jesus to be flow, the *substance* of God, from God. How does this reality impact your faith?

2. Does your life reflect the *dependent flow* Jesus modeled? Take time to listen for the Spirit's peaceful voice of guidance.

3. Look around for God's *prodigal* flow - reckless, extravagant divine love that shows no favoritism. Embrace it for yourself and ask God to reveal to you how to love others with prodigal love.

4

The Flow Within

Indeed, truly believing in Jesus, and therefore living
in him, means also living in God, i.e., living in that
flow of life that Jesus shares with his Father.
This makes all other kinds of living seem unreal.
Demetrius R. Dumm

Ancient Celtic Christians are known for their passionate
holistic spirituality including intimate community and deep
connection with nature. They believed the spiritual realm
remained closely connected with the physical realm. God was
near, always. The two realms touched at "thin times" and in
"thin places." Thin times were communal times of celebration
and mourning, like weddings and funerals or time spent alone in
thin places. Thin places included mountains, wells, the homes of
faithful people, or places connected with Celtic history like the
Isle of Iona. Celtic Christians paid attention to these thin times
and places hoping to remain in these margins or on these edges
so they might experience the spiritual and the physical world
simultaneously.[76]

Closer than near, God permeates and saturates. Every
place and time is *thin*. Sacred flow embraces life in the margins
or on the edges, but recognizes every time and place as thin.
God's incarnation through Christ has made every time and place
thin, so thin in fact that no boundary exists. We are *one* with
Jesus who serves as the gate, the gatekeeper, and the key to each
realm. It's God's vastness juxtaposed with our puny human
capacity (and religiosity) that projects the sense of thickness or
distance between us. It's time for our perception of separation to
vaporize.

49

becoming a pragmystic

A bitter irony exists in typical Christian communities today. Ministries and individuals alike spend a lot of time, money, and passion attempting to get their faith community or themselves "closer to God." Too much time is spent wallowing in, and perpetuating a culture of guilt and shame rather than embracing and exploring the reality of union with God and its applications. Instead of moving out into the community as ministers of reconciliation, most time is spent trying to *get* what is *already* possessed. A. W. Tozer spoke to this irony more than a half a century ago,

> God dwells in His creation and is everywhere indivisibly present in all His work. This is boldly taught by prophet and apostle and is accepted by Christian theology generally. That is, it appears in the books, but for some reason it has not sunk into the average Christian's heart so as to become a part of his believing self. Christian teachers shy away from its full implications, and, if they mention it at all, mute it down till it has little meaning.[77]

You may have driven past a church sign displaying a statement like this, "If you feel distant from God, who moved?" Obviously God did not move away, so the separation is your doing. Or maybe God pulled back since your behavior was so disgraceful. Many would say it is presumptuous, even arrogant to assume we have arrived with regard to a sustained union with God. We subtly believe that if we don't feel it, then it's not real. Our perception of intermittent separation lingers despite our affirmation of God's unconditional indwelling presence. Because we don't *feel* this union every moment does not preclude its reality.

The idea of his Christians 'getting closer to God' is redundant. Jesus tells his friends, "When I am raised to life again, you will know that I am in my Father, and you are in me, and I am in you."[78] We have ingested the flow and he has ingested us. We house God and God houses us. He envelops us like the air and permeates us like the water in our cells. This intimate God-union explains our ability to exude his life-giving fragrance.[79] Jesus brought union, a union to be experienced, celebrated, and shared with others.

> *We live and move in him, can't get away from him!*
> *Acts 17: 28*

The natural longing we have to *get closer to God* is better articulated as our desire for a more explicit awareness and experience of the union we already possess. The biblical assertion to draw near to God so that he will draw near to us speaks to experienced union rather than spiritual-spatial proximity. We need to practice living into the reality of God's indwelling presence despite what we feel or don't feel, do or don't do. Sacred flow nurtures this 'presence' practice.

Christianity has a great deal of mystery and mysticism embedded in its theology and practice. Historically, Christian mystics have sought to live by the Spirit, experiencing God's indwelling presence moment by moment. For centuries mystics have devoted their time and focus to directly experiencing the Source of all things. Unfortunately, most of our renowned mystics are dead or tucked away in monasteries. In the mainstream, Christian spirituality has been mostly de-mysticized. On the one hand, we give lip service to life in the Spirit, but our day to day Christian life is more about a restrictive set of behaviors. On the other hand, life in the Spirit is used to excuse all kinds of erratic over-emotionalism.

Many Christians today consign mysticism to the New Age movement, Eastern religions, or questionable expressions of contemporary Christianity. The word itself may conjure up uncomfortable imagery. We may believe mysticism necessitates dim lighting, candles, incense, chanting, or out of body experiences. Even if we think of Christian mystics as neat, intriguing, devoted people, we tend to relegate them to the fringes. Mysticism seems too eccentric, spiritually volatile, or uncontrollable to

> However far we may be drawn into the divine spaces opened up to us by Christian mysticism, we never depart from the Jesus of the Gospels. On the contrary, we feel a growing need to enfold ourselves ever more firmly within his human truth.
> *Pierre Teilhard de Chardin*

give it ground in the center of Christian spirituality.

Sacred flow calls us back into Christian mystery and mysticism. If we are going to truly experience the sacred flow of Jesus we must be familiarized or re-familiarized with Christian mysticism. In reality, the Christian mystic means to tap into God's divine life every day. She embraces the death and resurrection of Jesus and desires to live empowered by his Spirit. Certainly, experiencing and expressing God can be uncontrollable, uncomfortable, and volatile, sometimes lead us to the fringe.

Providing a brief history and description of Christian mysticism will be helpful. At the root of the term mysticism is mystery; in both its origin and definition. The term mystery, *mysterion* in Greek, refers to a secret, a mystery, to shutting one's mouth.[80] Mystics intentionally and intensely probe the mystery that is God. Broadly, the full identity and availability of God and the extent of his participation with us are this mystery's content.

Insight into this mystery lies at the depths of the written word of God. A read through does not suffice. Christian mystics desire and demand more than a read through and legalistic following of the biblical text. They desire to experience the full embrace offered by the text's author. Mystics believe the biblical text offers a glimpse of a flowing, actively creating God. The text serves as a foundation, a guide, and a diving board. Inanimate biblical text supernaturally inspires and empowers when truly illuminated by the Light of all things.

Two other themes along with mystery have dominated Christian mysticism: union and love. Mystics desire and seek God and his love through union. Love serves as mysticism's goal, method, and result. We fully apprehend love through experienced union with God. As we experience loving union with God we are compelled to love without restraint in an untold number of practical ways.

Divine mystery, union, and love cannot be realized without divine presence. Christian mysticism depends wholly upon God's presence. Mystics desire to directly experience and express the intimate presence of God. God's presence provides an opportunity and expectation for spiritual discovery. This discovery transforms them again and again as they continually seek to know God, his presence, and their authentic selves in light of his presence.

The Christian faith claims that the resurrected Son of God lives within us individually and corporately. His living Spirit teaches, guides, counsels, and comforts us from the inside and out. Equally mystical and mysterious, God has placed his followers in himself. In his letter to the Colossians, Paul explains that they have died

> **The mystics are artists; and the stuff in which they work is most often the human life.**
> *Evelyn Underhill*

(spiritually) and their real life is hiding with Christ inside God.[81] We are present to heaven and earth every moment of our existence. Experiencing and expressing this mutual indwelling here on earth serves as the core of Christian spirituality. Ours is a mystical faith no matter how we attempt to rationalize, normalize, or humanize it. You've likely heard the following before, but it bears repeating here: *to be a Christian is to be a mystic.*

Embracing mysticism will benefit our faith in incalculable ways. For it to do so, we need to embrace it in the midst of our everyday life. Our mysticism needs to be married to pragmatism. I call this *pragmysticism* and we who practice it *pragmystics*. We are pragmatic mystics. We simultaneously embrace and engage our everyday life and the supernatural presence of God in and around us.

Jesus was a *pragmystic*. He lived a practical human life fully attuned to the divine. Regretably, many people limit his mysticism to ecstatic experiences like the descending dove and the voice of God at his baptism or his transfiguration. Jesus' pragmysticism was rooted in the attention he paid to his Father moment by moment coupled with his daily encounters with people. He flowed from the Father in everything he did and didn't do. He deeply cared for people. He did very natural activities (and supernatural activities) while being guided and empowered in an extraordinary way.

The Apostle Paul was a pragmystic. We witness his pragmatism in his letters to churches offering specific encouragement, advice, and correction regarding daily life as a follower of Jesus. Nonetheless, the foundation of his pragmatism was mysticism. As with Jesus, we often relegate Paul's mysticism to a couple of ecstatic experiences, instead of a way of life he modeled, wrote about, and hoped to pass on to others.

53

The bulk of Paul's writing in the New Testament connects a mystical Jesus with his followers and teaches what can easily be interpreted as a pragmystical way of life.

Paul himself experienced sacred flow. He grasped the mysticism of Jesus, embodied it, and passed it on. He asserted that to live was Christ, that God willed and acted in him, and that his life was hidden with Christ in God. He said that by faith Christ lived through him, and that he strained according to the power of Christ within him.[82] All of these concepts are inherently mystical, rhythmic, and serve as cornerstones of

> **Authentic Christian mysticism is nothing but a living of the Gospel at a deep level of consciousness.**
> **William Johnston**

Christianity. Christian mystics throughout the ages have cherished and used Paul's writing to support their mystical theology and practical experience.

We are meant to be pragmystics. We have one foot in divine mystery and the other in earthly affairs. Jesus declares that we, like him, are in the world but not of it. We are to live consciously aware of God's enveloping presence as we do all that we do in this world. Pragmysticism is a way of life in the mundane as much as anywhere else. It recognizes our transcendent-immanent God in the practical: lunch break, bathing our kids, going for a jog, reading a book, camping, having coffee with a friend, commuting, and even in boring meetings. Our pragmysticism allows us to live miraculously even through the mundane patches of our lives.[83]

A *pragmystical* perception of spirituality leads us to engage the mystery of our union with God (and other mysteries) as part of our daily life. We will never nail these mysteries down, but that's not the point. Wrestling with these unfathomable mysteries serves as much needed cardiovascular exercise. Our heart needs the workout. We rhythmically engage, ponder, and process what it means to be indwelt by God, and vice versa as we go about life. We grapple with what it means to experience God in each moment and have Christ live his life through ours uniquely, especially during times of pain, persecution, or suffering. Our pragmysticism works itself out in the flow of the Spirit, a flow that is far more ordinary, intentional, and intuitive, than ecstatic.

embodying the Jesus life

Re-incarnation provides the foundation for our pragmystic way. By re-incarnation I am referring to our need to re-cognize or rethink our mutual incarnation with Jesus. Jesus incarnates us and we incarnate him. To incarnate means to *embody*, to *exemplify*, or to *personify*. Incarnation transforms the abstract into the concrete; in our case, the embodiment of a super and natural God.[84] Jesus, *the* incarnation of God, made God real to us. Through flesh and blood, he personified and exemplified the nature, character, and will of God. God the abstract became God the tangible and touchable.

We are real, concrete human beings, meant to express the nature, character, and will of God. We are the ongoing remnant of Jesus. God means to manifest himself through us in tangible ways. No, we're not Jesus, but we possess his Spirit and his Spirit possesses us. Re-collecting incarnation means re-collecting our true identity. Our authentic self welcomes the leadership of the Spirit of God within. We recollect our identity in rhythm with God's indwelling Spirit. Incarnating Christ means giving ourselves to a lifestyle in which we are flowing along empowered by God and bearing edible fruit.

We need daily re-cognition of two mysterious incarnations. First, Jesus' life was the embodied life of God. Secondly, Jesus has taken up residence in us and our life is meant to be a creative embodiment of his.[85] The gospel writer John tells us that those who say Jesus is God's son abide in God and God in them.[86] Christ was planted in this world, we were planted in him, and he in us. These dynamic incarnations represent the whole gospel, and thus supply a foundation for our sacred flow.

planted in Christ

Some years ago my parents purchased a condominium on a beach in Florida. In doing so, they included my sisters and me as "owners" with reference to the Condo Association. As owners, (by virtue of our parents) we retained the same rights and privileges as they did but without paying for them. My parents paid the price, and we reaped the benefits. Our relationship with the management at the Condo was the same as our parents. My sisters and I simply had to receive our

55

ownership. This was weird for the first few visits to the condo. I walked into a fully furnished condo and thought to myself, "I am an owner of 4E...this is my couch...this is my silverware...that is my boogie board...this is my view of the ocean...that is my parking spot, etc." It was surreal and really humbling. My only reasonable response was to receive the gift, be thankful, and use it responsibly. My parents were happy to include us. By being their son, being included "in them" I was one with them as an owner of 4E despite having not paid anything.

This concept holds true for us *in* Christ. Our being put into Christ provides us with all of the rights, relationships, privileges, and benefits Jesus possesses. Jesus becomes what we need when we need it. God put us into Christ and Christ became our wisdom, rightness, change agent, holiness, and rescuer.[87] Our being placed into Jesus' death and resurrection provided a way for us to exist in perfect unconditional union with the God. Jesus becoming separate from God, literally becoming the problem, allowed us to become whole and wholly united with God.

> *For He made Him who knew no sin to be sin for us,*
> *that we might become the righteousness of Christ in Him.*
> *2 Corinthians 5: 21*

Jesus became our representative wrongdoer and provided us with his "rightness." Thus, we became as "right" with God as Jesus. His rightness returned us to our rightful place.[88] No longer sinners by nature, we are holy ones, forgiven, united, and free. As Paul writes to the Corinthians, we are *one spirit with him.*[89] Spiritual dualism ended when Jesus removed everything that separated humanity from God.

In his letter to the Romans and Galatians, Paul articulates when and how we are placed into Christ.[90] Mysteriously, we too were crucified, buried, and raised from the dead with Christ. Our crucifixion and resurrection *with* Christ made way for our complete union and new way of life.

> *Or do you not know that all of us who have been baptized*
> *into Christ Jesus have been baptized into His death?*
> *Therefore we have been buried with Him through baptism*

> *into death, so that as Christ was raised from the dead*
> *through the glory of the Father, so we too might walk in*
> *newness of life. For if we have become united with Him*
> *in the likeness of His death, certainly we shall also be in the*
> *likeness of His resurrection, knowing this, that our old*
> *self was crucified with Him, in order that our body of sin*
> *might be done away with, so that we would no longer be slaves*
> *to sin; for he who has died is freed from sin. Now if we have*
> *died with Christ, we believe that we shall also live with Him.*
> *Romans 6: 5-8*

The concept of being *crucified with* Christ in the Greek, *sustauroo*, means to impale in company with.[91] Also, this crucifixion with Christ is written in the aorist tense in Greek meaning the event was a past occurrence with lasting effect.[92] Paul's crucifixion had already happened as he wrote, but the effects are eternal. Therefore, he considered himself dead – crucified with Christ, and would not go about attempting to crucify himself again and again. Just as he mysteriously died, he mysteriously rose to a new life in Christ.

Paul writes of being baptized into Christ's death and even being buried with him. The primary definition of the Greek term *baptizo* is "to make whelmed," immerse completely, to dunk.[93] We are dunked into Christ's death. Taking this figuratively, the act of baptism provides a meaningful metaphor. Considering this spiritually, we were mystically immersed into Christ and his death. The word picture related to being united with Jesus *in the likeness of his death* is that of being planted together.[94] The idea is that of being grown along with, closely united, fused, related in nature, firmly united, associated in birth or origin, being in close accord, congenial, or being of the same birth.[95] Followers of Christ were mysteriously placed on the cross and then in the ground with Christ. This co-planting initiates a union that is paradoxically complete and growing.

> **He is more within us than we are ourselves.**
> *Elizabeth Ann Seton*

Just as we were crucified with Jesus we were also raised with him. He carries us out of death into a new life, real life…his life. Paul writes to the Ephesians that Christ followers have been raised up, resurrected with and in Christ.

But God's mercy is great, and he loved us very much.
Though we were spiritually dead because of the things
we did against God, he gave us new life with Christ. You
have been saved by God's grace. And he raised us up
with Christ and gave us a seat with him in the heavens.
He did this for those in Christ Jesus.
Ephesians 2: 4-6

Paul claims that we are seated with God, in Christ, in heavenly places even as we live and breathe on earth. Somehow we are here and there simultaneously. What a strange hope-filled mystery. It's our faith that holds onto this union and leads us to live empowered by it despite not being able to wrap our minds around it. God has taken us into himself…an astonishing provision.

Christ planted in us

In 1990 researchers throughout the world immersed themselves in the Human Genome Project. The project set out to determine the sequencing of human DNA and classify the approximately 25,000 genes in the humane genome. The completed findings of the project were

The soul is in God and God is in the soul as a fish is in the sea and the sea in a fish.
Catherine of Siena

published in 2003 with additional findings continuing to be published today. This was and is one of the greatest undertakings in modern science. The overarching hope is that by gaining this knowledge, doctors will be able to influence genes and therefore cure and prevent diseases, as well as enhance our general well-being. Ultimately, the project will accomplish this by influencing a person's physical innermost, their fundamental blueprint.

Altering someone's genes alters them from the inside out. Whatever is changed in their fundamental code could manifest itself in a myriad of external ways. It might affect seemingly inconsequential superficial characteristics such as eye or hair color. However, it may be as consequential as saving a person's life if the altered genes prevent a fatal disease from germinating. Additionally, gene alteration may prevent psychological ills. If developed responsibly, these alterations made at our deepest physical level could save us or significantly alter our life for the better.

God has recreated and rejuvenated our spiritual genome. He has altered our innermost. He has injected his divine *Gene* into us. This genetic renewal and saturation carries with it substantial far-reaching consequences. This genetic rebirth and continual enhancement finds its way into much of our practical life. It doesn't modify our physical genes but affects how we live from them. More specifically, our spiritual genetics may advise which jeans we wear and where we go while wearing them. It doesn't alter our eye color but certainly how we appreciate and use our eyes.

God shrouded this spiritual genome project in mystery for ages, alluding to it in the writings of the prophets. Its specific timing, shape, and manifestation remained a secret. Expectation soared but true understanding was minimal. Paul discloses the mystery in his letter to the Colossians.

> *Of this church I was made a minister according to the stewardship from God bestowed on me for your benefit, so that I might fully carry out the preaching of the word of God, that is, the mystery which has been hidden from the past ages and generations, but has now been manifested to His saints, to whom God willed to make known what is the riches of the glory of this mystery among the Gentiles, which is **Christ in you**, the hope of glory.*
> *Colossians 1: 25-27*

This mystery proves fundamental and far-reaching. The mystery, or at least a portion of it, is as Paul clearly states, "Christ in you." This was and is beyond what anyone could have imagined – Yahweh embedded, inborn, indwelling.

Messiah has come to dwell in us. The term *in* found here in Colossians is a primary preposition indicating a *fixed location*.[96] Christ is fixed in us. This fixation is even more profound and compassionate considering our continuing stumbles, foibles, and failures. Even the worst behaved followers, despite their reprehensible behavior, house God's Spirit. In his personal letter to the Corinthians, Paul calls this badly behaving bunch saints. Their activity is reprehensible but it doesn't define them, God does. He reminds them (and us) that God has purchased them and therefore they are the physical temples of their indwelling God. This being the case, they are to act like it.[97]

Paul's incarnation statement in Colossians – Christ in you – resonates with a prophecy given by Ezekiel about six hundred years prior. God foretold his plan to embed himself in us. The prophet Ezekiel announced that God would make a new covenant with his people. In this new agreement the people would be made spiritually new, injected with God's Spirit, and led from within.

> *Then I will sprinkle clean water on you, and you will be clean; I will cleanse you from all your filthiness and all your idols. Moreover, I will give you a new heart (with new and right desires) and put a new spirit within you; and I will remove the heart of stone (your heart of sin) from your flesh and give you a (new) heart of flesh (soft obedient heart). I will put My Spirit within you and cause you to walk in my Statutes and you will be careful to obey my ordinances (do whatever I ask).*
> *Ezekiel 36: 25-27[98]*

According to Ezekiel, God would provide a spiritual cleansing, a new spiritual identity, a new heart, and His Spirit. First, all of our sin and idol worship would be forgiven and taken away by the sacrifice of Jesus. God means to replace anything and everything we idolize or prioritize above him. An idol is an image. Whatever images we have pursued to bring us wholeness will be replaced by God himself. God becomes our idol, priority, image, and life. Our new spiritual identity is both right and righteous.

The heart serves as the center of everything we consider our soul. It's the inseparable mixture of our personality, emotions, will, and intellect.[99] God-responsive hearts replace our stony untrustworthy hearts. The deceitful heart that the prophet Jeremiah and other religious leaders have warned us about has been replaced with a soft God-responsive one.[100] We no longer need to live in fear of our heart. God has renewed the center of our soul. We are meant to live freely and boldly from our new heart. Sure, we will make mistakes, but we'll learn and grow in the process. Our new heart is naturally drawn to the sacred flow of God's Spirit.

Finally, the prophecy claims God will send his Spirit to dwell within us so we will do what he leads us to do. God's indwelling Spirit will *cause* us to walk in his ways. This speaks to how we are to live in our new relationship with God. Remarkably, God has taken it upon himself to empower us to move according to his will. This is the essence of empowering grace. Ezekiel's prophecy addresses how God deals with our wayward spirit, sin-saturated souls, and impulsive humanness. He promises to recreate, renovate, resource, and redirect us.

I've heard other Christians say that we are like the moon reflecting the sun. There is nothing inherently good about us; we just reflect the perfect light of the Son. God's light hits us, bounces off, and thus we give his light to others. We're only meant to be the best reflectors we can be. I disagree.

This idea only relates a small portion of what God has done through Jesus. More than simply reflecting Sonlight, we emanate and refract it. God has taken us from deep space darkness into his marvelous light. He has made us worthy and put his light within us. Unlike the moon, we aren't dead celestial bodies. We are living mini-sons (and daughters). We are not God, but we are God's offspring. More than reflection, we emanate his light from within. Rather than simply deflecting God's light, we refract it. When his light flows into and through our soul-cracks, it bends, turns, and twists. God's uses our imperfection to kaleidoscope his redemptive light into colorful rays that light up those who surround us.

> **Christ enters the poverty of our self-enclosed selves, indwells us, and makes his divine life to be our own.**
> *Miroslav Volf*

***

Last chapter established Jesus as the *Logos-flow* of God and our model flow-er. Our profound connection with him allows us to experience his flow with the Father. Following his lead, as Christians we are meant to live as pragmystics. We give attention to the mystical and the practical simultaneously. We continually acknowledge God's presence while looking to experience him in the midst of our daily doings. God made this possible by planting us in him and him in us. We have been made new, united with God, and injected with an empowering Spirit. This provides a solid foundation for a flowing faith.

I acknowledge that our union with God, its inter-workings, and its implications are great mysteries. As you read this chapter you may have dismissed my expression or explanation of God in Christ as too mystical, out of touch, and far-fetched…or too literal, technical, and reductionist. I understand. It seems impossible or absurd that God himself has not only recreated our spirit but also eternally enmeshed his Spirit with ours. Rightly so, we will wrestle with these mysteries and their weight throughout our lives.

The truth is that the treasure lies within our very selves.
Teresa of Avila

Our faith bridges the gap. We take a significant but worthy risk by *faithing* what was shared in this chapter. We are one with God. And through the power of the Spirit we can flow with the Father as Jesus did. By faith, we lean into God's love, mystery, paradox, and flow.

The just shall live by flow… God's flow.

being formed by God's flow

1. How is your life lacking *pragmystic* balance? Consider if you rely too much on the *super* to the point of superstition or passivity, or if you rely too much on the *natural,* leaning toward independence and self-reliance.
2. Spend some time meditating on your mutual indwelling with God. Contemplate what it means to be and to live *in* God. Also, reflect upon what it means for Christ to live *in* you.
3. Ponder God's flow within you as you read through Paul's letter to the Romans.

5

Our Freedom to Flow

The Holy Spirit, the very voice of Divine Liberty, must
always be like the wind in "blowing where he pleases." In the
mystery of the Old Testament there was already a tension
between the Law and the Prophets. In the New Testament
the Spirit himself is the Law, and he is everywhere.
Thomas Merton

Just after the turn of the century I faced the most
overwhelming challenge I've faced in my life thus far... no, I'm
not talking about distributing 3000 cans of beef stew left over
after an uneventful Y2K. I still have those in my bunker. In
reality, as a twenty-seven year old counselor-pastor with a wife
and a baby daughter I was selling or giving away everything I
owned to in order to move to Eastern Europe. The related stress
could have easily crushed me. I was moving to Czech Republic
to start a ministry and I didn't speak more than three words of
the Czech language. Even more challenging, Czech Republic
ranked as one of the most atheistic countries in the world. I faced
raising funds for my salary, the move, in-country set up, and
ongoing ministry costs. Additionally, my wife and I still owed a
sizable amount of money for our student loans. Local support in
Czech would come from a small international church in Prague;
thus we would be going without a team. As for our departure
timetable, we needed to finish preparations, raise all the
required funding, pack, and leave in five months.

What was I thinking?

Prior to experiencing God's flow, my insecurities would
have dominated me, causing untold consequences that would
have likely prevented our move to Czech and done irreparable

damage to my soul and likely, my marriage. My religiosity had two faces, proud and puny. It would have prodded me to proudly do the most and best I could for God. On the other hand, I would have felt puny, unworthy, and inadequate for the task at hand. I would have been paralyzed by my fear of failing God, my church, my family, and myself. The height and weight of the obstacles we faced would have likely overwhelmed me. I would have been on the verge of implosion. My pride would have had me deny and bury my pain while pushing forward with *my* plan for God's sake.

Despite all of this, it's possible that my perfectionism and desire for control would not have allowed me to fully entertain the whole idea in the first place. As a young pastor with a good heart, I mostly focused upon survival in my performance-driven lifestyle. This overseas sojourn moved me toward a deep-seated faith, one well beyond superficial religious rhetoric. Prior to wading out into God's sacred flow, the depth of my faith was suspect.

We moved to Prague. Everything that needed to happen happened and we moved. Thankfully, I faced these overwhelming circumstances (funding, logistics, debt, short timeline, language barrier, lack of team, etc.) as I was learning to fully lean into God's flow. Granted, it was not long after I discovered sacred flow that I faced all this, but I had come into a new way of approaching life. These circumstances were beyond me and I knew it. I was in so deep over my head that I couldn't see the surface. I learned to trust God to live through me as I dealt with each challenge. I had nothing to prove so I simply relied on God to come through. I became free to risk. If God desired for us to go, he would take care of these overwhelming circumstances. God would make a way as I showed up each day and trusted in his grace and guidance. I learned what it means to flow freely, restfully, and expectantly despite my circumstances.

During our years in Prague we continued to face daunting challenges. The culture and language continually confounded us. Working alone in an unfamiliar culture is a formidable task, much less starting an organization in one. I wasn't always well received, nor was the message of God's grace that I shared. At times we felt vulnerable as American expatriates in Europe in a post 9-11 world. During our second year abroad our toddler had a massive seizure and local doctors diagnosed her with epilepsy. Thankfully, she didn't have it. My wife suffered several miscarriages. In an odd accident, our infant son was badly scalded with hot coffee in a restaurant. In general, we wrestled with feelings of loneliness and isolation. Utter dependence upon God's sacred flow got us through all this and more without sinking. We went

The moment I turn to God it is like turning on an electric current which I feel through my whole being.
Frank Laubach

under on many occasions, but each time we bobbed back to the surface. We were learning to embrace our freedom to flow.

God's strength becomes most real to us in the midst of our utter hopelessness.[101] We can't fully experience God's grace without first coming to grips with our brokenness. There is no resurrection without death. In our weakness we're better able to perceive the inadequacy of our self-strength and engage God's grace-strength. We trust our infinite Source to lead us and come through for us rather than constantly relying upon whatever we can muster. The way of will power is not the way of freedom.

Chapter three detailed Jesus' modeling of a new way of being and doing in which he flowed with the Father. The last chapter described our perfect union with Jesus and his empowering presence that sets us up to flow as he did. To better understand how to experience God's flow in our daily lives is crucial. For this, we must understand and embrace our freedom to flow. Jesus established our freedom to flow by establishing a new Law. Jesus himself is this new law. We're meant to flow in his Spirit.

free at last

My Counsel is this: live freely,
animated and motivated by God's Spirit.
Galatians 5: 16, The Message

I've been told that many laws exist to regulate the treatment of children by their parents. They establish a baseline level of parenting. They're meant to provide a safe environment for children, protecting them from various forms of neglect and abuse. I am a parent with three children, and I don't know any of these laws. I don't need them. I love my children dearly. I would lay my life down for them. The love I have for my children guides my actions well above and beyond requirement of the law.[102]

The love of God expressed in the person Jesus and now through us generates this effect. Living and loving is this manner goes well beyond any legal or moral code. Jesus (re)established God's Law of love by setting us free to focus upon God rather than religious rules. Jesus was a game changer. The Scriptures say Jesus set us free from sin and the Law. We are encouraged to consider, count, deem, or comprehend ourselves as such.[103]

Essentially, Jesus saved us from ourselves. Sin is self-sourcing. Living sinfully is what the Bible calls "living according to the flesh." Fleshly living is guided by human appetite. The question, "How can I get my needs met (now) apart from God?" compels our behavior. Even when our intentions are honorable this goes poorly. In an effort to please God, we draw upon our sheer will power to follow the Law of God. We cannot measure up this way. This easily results in a dreadful cycle of striving, self-righteousness, guilt, and shame – the Sisyphus system. God's Law expresses God's perfection and always proves our imperfection.

God has set us free from this lifestyle. He set us free from the externally-driven life. Jesus turned religion inside out. Sin and the Law both work outside in. Typically, when we sin we are looking for externals that will meet our internal needs. Turning to God's Law, an external ordinance, we try our best (with God's help) to follow his rules. With God embedded, we no longer have to live this way.

Jesus set us free from the prison of self-sourcing. Our being planted in Christ freed us from the need to self-source. Sure, we may return to it but we no longer have to do so as a way of life. God stepped in to provide us with himself as our Source. Sin no longer defines us, and it doesn't have to drive our behavior. The Spirit of God means to direct and empower every aspect of our life. We're free to live in the flow of the Spirit.

Unfortunately, most Christians are living under religious law, a former way. I have spent my fair share of time there and still do from time to time. We have taken onto ourselves the Mosaic Law given specifically to the Israelites. These laws weren't meant for the contemporary non-Jew. By

Mosaic Law I mean the Ten Commandments plus the other six hundred or so ordinances that follow.

This assimilation of the law was a pressing issue in the earliest days of Christianity. Should non-Jews be circumcised? Should they become Jews before becoming followers of Jesus? Should they keep the Law that defined Israel as a people? Eventually, the leaders of the church officially discussed this in Jerusalem and it's recorded in the book of Acts, chapter fifteen. After the discussion, they said it seemed right to them and the Holy Spirit to not *burden* the non-Jew with the Law. This resulted in a reduction of the whole Law to a few abstinences. They were told to abstain from food sacrificed to idols, sexual immorality, meat of strangled animals, and from blood. These activities were related to the worship of pagan gods. Essentially, non-Jew converts were asked to surrender particular practices, believe in Jesus, and live by God's Spirit.

> **The place in which we are invited to dwell is infinitely mysterious center of the Covenant, for Jesus Christ is the Covenant.**
> *Hans Urs Von Balthasar*

Jesus set us completely free. The Apostle Paul expresses this to the Christians in Corinth. Anything they want to do or not do is permissible. God's grace can't be trumped by our poor choices. They are totally and eternally forgiven and free. But Paul reminds them that not all choices are beneficial. Not all choices edify or enlighten. Not all choices reflect who they have become in relationship with God. Also, poor choices don't come without consequences. Sin always leads to the stink of death in some form or another. God's Spirit never empowers poor choices. God inspires us to use our freedom to make choices that benefit and uplift everyone.

Jesus set a new standard for Jews and non-Jews alike. As Jesus himself says, rather than negate God's law he fulfills it. He creates a higher code. He explains this by offering a simple statement that encompasses all that was given through Moses and what is expected going forward; *love God with all that you are and possess and your neighbor as yourself.* This goes beyond the Law that God had granted. The chief characteristic of this love is sacrifice and it reaches further than actions to the intentions of the heart. It doesn't betray the Mosaic Law but gives it deeper expression and integration within humanity. In Jesus' day religion had twisted and modified the simplicity and depth of what God desired from people. Jesus reestablished the simplicity and depth of God's expectation – love. God's indwelling Spirit means to empower us to love God, others, and ourselves with divine intensity.

This love-law was established through the New Covenant in Christ. In Jewish tradition, new law between God and humanity came through covenant. We don't have much context for covenants in our culture today outside of the marriage covenant. Unfortunately, in this case it has lost much of its meaning as more than half of all marriages, Christians notwithstanding, end in divorce.

Covenants are more significant than a simple agreement or contract. Covenants in Jewish culture were extremely serious, nothing less than sacred. The term comes from the Hebrew *berith*, meaning "to bind or fetter; a binding obligation."[104] The covenant often represented the ultimate expression of unconditional love between two parties. It signified two parties fusing together, becoming one, and establishing themselves in league with one another forever. Covenants also represented a treaty-like agreement established between a dominant nation or tribe and a much weaker one. The more powerful group established a covenant agreeing to integrate rather than annihilate the weaker one.

> **The triumph of grace enables people to live their ordinary lives divinely.**
> *Thomas Keating*

Covenants were cut, literally. Ceremonially, the two parties, with arms or hands cut and bound together, walked as one through the blood of a sacrifice that was split in half and laid out on the ground. It was a bloody affair. Altogether, covenant making required representatives from two parties, a mediator, a sacrifice to be split, and promises or laws. The parties established and spoke promises detailing their commitment to one another. The ceremony ended with a celebration including a covenant feast.

God, through Jesus, mediated a new eternal covenant with us. Jesus embodied all of the mediating roles. He was a perfect representative of God and of humanity, the eternal priest-mediator, the perfect eternal sacrifice, and the new eternal law.[105] He was God and human, a perfect representation of both.

In order to make the covenant, the best of God and humanity was put forth. The incarnation of Jesus allowed him serve as God's representative, our representative, and as the blood sacrifice.

The letter to the Hebrews points to Jesus' uniqueness as our eternal perfect priest. Jesus always lives to advocate and intercede for us. The writer of Hebrews informs us that there were great numbers of priests in the former covenant because death prevented them from perpetually interceding on behalf of the people. They just kept dying. They may have done a great job of interceding on behalf of the Jewish community for a season but they were only human. They were imperfect men offering temporal sacrifices for a temporary forgiveness. On the other hand, Jesus' eternal sinless flow with the Father qualified him to mediate himself for us forever. Jesus was fathered by God, appointed by God, made perfect forever, and came after the Law in order to establish an unending covenant of grace with us.[106]

Jesus' served as a suffering sacrifice once to take away sins of the past, present, and future. This is a vast improvement on the prior agreement in which sacrifices needed to continually be made in order to *cover* wrongdoing. Once a year the priests ceremonially carried out God's instructions to cover the sins of the people. Then comes Jesus, the blameless Lamb of God who *takes away* the sins of the world. He removed sins, literally *lifted them up*. Another powerful representative image here is that of *sailing away*. Jesus sailed away our sins. The letter to the Hebrews says that he did so by offering his untainted blood once on heaven's original altar, not an earthly facsimile. He appeared before God on our behalf to take care of this issue completely. This notion is radically different than constant sacrifice and constant asking of forgiveness for temporary covering.[107] Instead of continually confessing and asking God for forgiveness, we can admit our wrongdoing, thank God for the forgiveness he granted through Christ, and humbly move on with life. 'Bad' behavior is no longer an issue between God and us.

God's *new* covenant in Christ was new in that nothing like it had existed before. God had not related to his creation in the way that he would through the Jesus covenant. He would possess and move his people in a new way. Jesus' return home freed us to flow by granting us total forgiveness and mutual indwelling. This established him as our eternal internal promise keeper and the substance of our sacred flow. The New Covenant was an unthinkable dream – Yahweh…God unspeakable, un-writeable, and untouchable would now be entirely one with us.

How does this covenant concept fit into sacred flow? Remember, *covenants define relationships*. A new covenant means a new orientation for our relationship with God. In the former covenant God worked primarily outside in but now he works primarily inside out. The New Covenant flows…from within. Sacred flow is naturally suited for the orientation of our new agreement with God. We are tasked with humbly receiving and learning to live from God's radical provision from the inside out.

Elvis impersonators illustrate this outside in, inside out idea. Excellent Elvis impersonators not only master his look and voice; they are students of his life. They know the lyrics to all his songs, his movie roles, and his life story down to his favorite foods. Being a devoted student of Elvis would be helpful but still lacking. Taking it a step further, they could live by the credo, "WWED? – What would Elvis do?" Nonetheless, this impersonation is still pretending. It's an outside-in approach. Master impersonators can only create reputable yet hollow personifications.

To truly embody Elvis, they would need the actual spirit of Elvis to indwell them. This intimate internal union would make it possible for Elvis to live through them. They could learn to give Elvis' spirit free reign within them. Only an indwelling spirit would provide innermost identification and empowerment for an authentic personification. The New Covenant puts the Spirit of the living God in us to flow through us, from the inside out. Thank you…thank you very much.

The New Covenant changed the priesthood, and according to God's economy when the priesthood changes the law must change.[108] In opening his gospel, John discloses that the Law was given through Moses and grace and truth have been realized in Jesus.[109] The new Law *is* Jesus who embodies grace and truth. Jesus fulfilled the Law of Moses giving full expression to God's standard of holiness.[110] He fulfills and overshadows the former Law, leaving it to fade and become obsolete.[111] The Jesus Law creates a higher standard than the Law of Moses. The New Covenant fulfilled the Mosaic covenant in every way. He mediates a superior covenant, not because God or the Law was flawed, but because the people couldn't keep up their end of the agreement. They consistently betrayed their commitment (just as we would have).[112] God knew this would happen and graciously provided Jesus as a way forward for the Israelites and everyone else.

Jesus presents us a new way of thinking of Law. Paul writes to the Romans that Jesus was the end or the goal of the Law. He is not only the end of the Law, but he *is* the new Law. The Law becomes a person. Our death in Christ freed us from our relationship with the Law and united us with Jesus so that we could freely live for God via the Spirit.[113] We are not meant to be anti-Mosaic Law; we simply no longer have a relationship with it. We're one with Jesus and that's enough. He gives himself via the Holy Spirit as our Law within. God not only implants this higher Law, his presence naturally empowers our fulfillment of it.[114]

God's Law given by Moses proves our inadequacy and leads us to Jesus' grace-filled flow. Paul explains that law-living puts us under a curse since we cannot possibly keep the whole Law.[115] The curse of sin and the Law is death, an abiding sense of emptiness and separation. We will always fall short, feel shamed, and be guilt-ridden. Jesus bore our shortfall, shame, and guilt. He kept the Law and became cursed on our behalf in order to redeem and rescue us from sin and the Law.[116] The Law means to lead us freedom by way of Jesus.

> **He himself is the fuel our spirits were designed to burn, or the food our spirits were designed to feed on. There is no other.**
>
> *C.S. Lewis*

Paul writes to the Galatian community that the Law means to restrain us, protect us, break us, and leave us at the feet of the Jesus. From there, a faith that flows in God's Spirit is to become our new way of life. The Law kills but the Spirit gives life[117] The Sisyphus system kills but the sacred flow of the Spirit gives life. We may return to law-living anytime we like, but in a fool-proof manner the Law always breaks us and leads us back to Jesus. We're meant live solely by his Spirit.[118]

> *This is a covenant not of written laws, but of*
> *the Spirit. The old written covenant ends in death;*
> *but under the new covenant, the Spirit gives life.*
> 2 Corinthians 3: 6

We have been released into a new way of living, a new life principle, a new grace-filled flow. We are not released into a balancing act of law and grace but into grace alone. The spirit of grace is the spirit of Jesus. Grace *is* the gospel. Grace in action is Christ within us compelling us to love as he loves.

Not unlike our Christian communities today, the first century Galatian Christian community slid into mixing grace-living with law-keeping. It's easy to do. Paul wrote (as I am writing) to call us back into unadulterated grace, recognizing the indwelling Spirit of Christ as our Law of life. They were being duped by false teachers into law-keeping. In their context, this specifically concerned the need to be circumcised to be a follower of

Just as wherever birds fly they always encounter the air, so also wherever we go or wherever we are, we find God present.
Frances de Sales

Christ. Paul viscerally responds to this by saying he hopes these teachers of circumcision would mutilate or castrate themselves.

Freedom is no insignificant matter. We're set free to be free…to live, love, and serve others freely. The Law of Christ leads us to love with all that we are and possess, period. The whole Law is summed up in love.[119] So, the *doing* of the new Law of Christ comes down to wholly loving God, our neighbor, and our self. This *doing* is appropriated by faith and empowered by his Spirit.

Christ as our Source

Writer George Maloney asserts, "We Christians are raised to a new life by possessing a new principle of activity, Christ himself."[120] In like manner, Thomas Merton clearly and concisely states that Christ manifests himself in us by becoming our new source of life, identity, and method.[121] Christ is not in us to help us keep us in line, he *is* the keeper and the line. Jesus is much more than our personal assistant; he is our source of guidance and strength.

Referring again to the Old Testament prophet Ezekiel's foretelling of the New Covenant, he notes God saying, "I will put My Spirit within you and *cause* you to walk in My statutes, and you will be careful to observe My ordinances." God claims he will, by his Spirit, emphatically *cause* us to walk in his ways. The verb *cause* here means, "to do, make, bring about, work, produce, accomplish, or effect."[122]Jesus is our source, our cause, our principle of life, the substance of our flow bringing forth his ways. Jesus calls himself *the way*. He is the path, the street, the route, and even more dynamically he is our *mode* and *means*. The Spirit of sacred flow causes and compels us from within.

> *[Not in your own strength] for it is God Who is all the*
> *while effectually at work in you [energizing and*
> *creating in you the power and desire], both to will and*
> *to work for His good pleasure and satisfaction and delight.*
> *Philippians 2: 13, AMP*

To the Galatians Paul writes, "The life I live in the body, I live by faith in the Son of God…"[123] The old faithless Paul was slain at the cross, embedded in Jesus, and no longer directs his life. Christ became his way of life. The mystical presence of Christ lived in and through him. Christ didn't make Paul a puppet or nullify his personality, but fulfilled him. Paul became more Paul than ever before. In this new life he experienced peace and complete union with God and himself. He recognized that the Spirit of the living God served as his advocate, counselor, teacher, and source of strength. The same is true for us. Union with God has been accomplished and a boundless internal source made available to us. Christ is our life. Flowing in his Spirit is our way of life.

***

The New Covenant removed the two primary obstacles that blocked our union with God and our ability to flow: our inherent rebellion and self-sourced living. Through the New Covenant we receive Jesus' earthly relationship with the Father and as a result, the freedom to flow. Jesus is everything. We no longer have to live outside-in in accordance with a divine moral code or a self-induced humanistic code. We can live inside-out sourced by God himself. God means for us to use our inside-out freedom to love and serve others. Christ within us empowers us to do so.

We are encouraged to stand firmly in our grace-found freedom. A return to law-living betrays the sacrifice of Jesus and our opportunity to flow.[124] Remember, where the Spirit is, there is liberty...to flow.[125] Only freedom will allow us to fully trust God in every moment and therefore flow in his Spirit. Release yourself into freedom. God already has.

being formed by God's flow

1. Read slowly through Hebrews chapters 7-10. Ask God to reveal his grace covenant to you in new and fresh ways.
2. Meditate on Christ what it means to trust Christ to be your source moment by moment.
3. Take some time to reflect upon how you have lived under the Law rather than under grace. Celebrate your freedom by reading through Paul's letter to the Galatians.

The Second Current

Framing a Faith That Flows

*current: (noun) - something that flows as a river
or a stream.*

6

Focus

The Lord is *at* the center of your being; therefore,
He must *become* the center of your being.
Jeanne Guyon

So far in my semi-short life I've worked in a lot of
different roles and in diverse environments. Through my teen
and university years I bussed tables, worked in construction,
facilities, athletic training, landscaping, and worked on the
grounds crew for professional baseball and softball teams. Since
graduate school I've worked in the United States and abroad as a
coach, pastor, counselor, recruiter, and public speaker. Without
hesitation, I can say that the amount of satisfaction and success
that I experienced in all of these roles and environments
depended upon my level of focus.

Whether our daily work is as simple as cutting grass or
as complex as foreign diplomacy, focus matters. Giving full
attention to the task at hand and people who surround us
provides satisfaction, success, and oftentimes flow. This holds
true in our work, play, family life, and faith.

We often hear the CEO of an ailing company, the coach
of a struggling team, or the leader of a troubled country say,
"We need to return to our roots, and regain our focus." These
companies, teams, and countries lost sight of their source of
identity, strength, or values somewhere along the way. This
happens in our faith as well. Faith-roots are core to both the
physical and spiritual realm. We can easily lose sight of our
roots, get focused on the superficial, and hinder the fruit-bearing
of our faith. To experience a deep-grounded faith that flows, we

must live from our roots. Staying in touch with our roots keeps us connected with our foundation while we learn and grow.

The next three chapters express how our Christian spirituality integrates with flow's roots. As with Jesus, the root-components of flow integrate smoothly with us. Focus, challenge, and feedback provide a solid pragmystical foundation making way for our spiritual life to organically and authentically grow and flourish. They don't do so as a rigid religious structure but as a gracious wonder-filled framework facilitating a flowing relationship with God. The roots are just that: roots, not flow-*laws*. They are more like anchors meant to stabilize and refocus our faith. Paradoxically, it's these *anchors* that ready us to *flow*. The roots lead us back to our Source to experience deeper intimacy and divine rhythm. The roots lead us into God's rhythm and flow, his beat. They help us live there, and return there again and again.

Flow begins with focus. Focus serves as the taproot of the roots of sacred flow. Remember, flow *is* focus. Challenge and feedback cannot occur without focus. We can't tackle challenges of any consequence without staying focused. And feedback is useless if we're not focused enough to respond to it. Focus enables us to deeply engage activities, situations, and people. Deep engagement feeds flow.

concentration: tapping into the Source

During one of Jesus' visits to the home of Mary and Martha in Bethany, Mary sits close to Jesus concentrating on his every word. Martha becomes increasingly frustrated with Mary's disregard for her household duties. Martha asks Jesus to reprimand her. Jesus responds by saying something of this nature, "Only one thing is truly worth your attention, Mary has chosen it and I am not going to interrupt her."[126] This statement encourages Mary (and us) to intensely concentrate upon Jesus, his words and his ways. Our doing is meant to flow from our attentiveness to God. The 'one good thing' is to concentrate upon Jesus, the *Logos*. His Spirit reveals, revives, creates, and compels us. God serves as the focal point of a flowing faith. The cost of flowing in the Spirit is concentration.

Referring again to chapter two, to concentrate is to bridle our attention, to unify it. Concentration intentionally narrows our consciousness. Concentration is focus. Deep concentration in the context of our faith means recollecting the God-consciousness that we lost in life's last tussle; a tussle lasting ten seconds, ten minutes, or ten years. Turning to God sparks renewal and rhythm in our soul. English mystic Evelyn Underhill asserted that by simplification, removal of distraction, and turning to one's consciousness inward we can unite our rhythm with the rhythm of God.[127] Deep concentration re-orients God as our Source.

Ours is a Trinitarian concentration. By narrowing our focus to the Trinity, our world opens up. The mystery of the Father, Son, and the Holy Spirit being both divisible and indivisible supplies plenty of depth and breadth for our concentration. The term Trinity (perichoresis) is formed from the words *peri* meaning circle and *choreio* meaning dance. The Divine moves, flows, and dances in an interwoven and interdependent circle. This circle-dance has been dubbed "The Great Dance." In Christ we enter the Great Dance. What a powerful image! We dance amongst the Trinity in the midst of all our circumstances. This keeps our concentration "on its toes." The diverse situations that arise in our lives provide us with plenty of opportunities to concentrate on each person of the Trinity. We may find

> **Sin means that people are stepping out of the [Trinity's] dance, corrupting its beauty and rhythm, crashing and tackling and stomping on feet instead of moving with grace, rhythm and reverence. Then, in Jesus, God enters creation to restore the rhythm and beauty again.**
> *Brian D. McLaren*

ourselves pondering God's identity, character, will, way, or specific activity in a given situation. When we enter the vast expanse of God's perspective via the Father, Son, and Holy Spirit we more effectively live out God's fatherly and motherly love, Jesus' sacrificial compassion, and the Holy Spirit's incessant but gentle encouragement.

Concentration leads to faith, transformation, and oftentimes clarity. While concentrating or meditating upon God, we more clearly perceive him, who he has made us to be, and how he is leading us to live. Our concentration brings revelation, reorientation, re-imagination, redirection and re-empowerment.

In our Trinitarian concentration, God directs what, who, when, and where we are to give our attention in each moment. At some point you've tapped into the Source this way. You've sensed God was leading you to pray for a certain person at a certain time, to call them or meet with them and you didn't really know why. This may be a person that hasn't even entered your mind for a decade. Or, in a moment of stillness, you've sensed God inspiring you to give attention to something you've put off for weeks, months, or maybe even years. Maybe you had a hellacious Monday and at some point you paused, took a deep breath, and asked God to move you from flailing to focus…and He did. Quite regularly in specific moments I've sensed God nudging me to give my wife or kids a word of encouragement or a reassuring hug and kiss. Admittedly, it's difficult to go wrong responding to that particular spiritual nudge.

Researching for this book proved difficult. It was no small task to reframe Christian spirituality using flow as both a guiding metaphor and a framework. I found myself studying many directions and at varying depths in those directions. The Bible alone provides infinite depth and story for the task. A wealth of great content surfaced to study, and much of it I had to superficially skim. My primary desire was to trust God's direction with regards to when and where to concentrate my study, which stories or illustrations to use, and how to arrange everything. I intended to write moved by God's flow.

> **Attention is power…Attention is the singular act of creativity that is available to each of us every waking moment…We create ourselves by what we choose to notice.**
>
> *Lucy Jo Palladino*

Often, God doesn't reveal *why* he has directed our focus in a particular direction for a particular time. On countless occasions I have asked, *"God, what was that about?"* Many times this question comes during a time of confusion, pain, loss, or frustration. Specifically, I have posed this question when I have felt God directed me in an odd manner, or to a particular place where nothing of consequence seemed to occur. The peculiar direction may be brief, comical, catastrophic, or consume years of our life. Furthermore, we may harbor intense hurt and anger with God about moving us toward or away from a certain place or person. Or we may just be befuddled. The following two stories exemplify these situations and inspire the aforementioned question, *"God, what was that about?"*

I was really focused on doing something nice for my wife on our tenth wedding anniversary. What could be nicer than cruising the Caribbean in December? No kids, no cold weather, just the sun, gourmet food, margaritas, and Mexico. We dropped our kids off with their grandparents and drove excitedly to the port. We boarded the boat and immediately sensed a debacle. We got to our room and it smelled musty, like dirty wet socks. We soon learned that we were on the smallest, oldest ship in the fleet. Oh no. We pondered exiting the ship to stay in a nice local hotel. Instead, we stayed aboard…big mistake. It stormed the entire trip. The boat rocked for days as passengers lost their lunch and their footing. When it rains for three days on the smallest ship in the fleet, there is little to do but eat. To be expected on this ill-fated trip, the food was subpar and even worse, caused Montezuma's revenge. So, we spent most of our time watching television in our musty cabin. Fittingly, we watched the same *Pirates of the Caribbean* movie about four times. The icing on this rotten cake was that we weren't allowed to disembark in one of our ports due to weather and at the other port it rained the entire time we were ashore. At least the ship didn't sink. *God, what was that about?*

My friend Joseph loved filmmaking as a kid. Passionate about it throughout his teenage years, he majored in film at university. As a senior he was specially chosen from among his classmates to direct a short film. The film was good enough to be shopped around Hollywood in hopes of a directing job. Hollywood loved it but told him to make a feature length film in order to prove himself on a larger scale. So, Joseph did. It took five arduous years of focused fundraising, writing, directing, filming, editing, etc. He finished the film and returned to Hollywood. They loved the film…and without offering any future financing or a job they told him they couldn't wait to see his next one.

Joseph, exhausted and disappointed, decided to take a brief respite from filmmaking. The break led him back to his hometown where he took a job outside of the film industry. Within a week back in his hometown he met his future wife. A few months later they began dating, in less than a year they were married, and not much later became parents. Having transitioned careers and coasts, gaining a wife and two children, happy with the outcome, he still sometimes scratches his head in thought about his prolonged filmmaking quest. *God, what was that about?*

Granted, these examples are pretty innocuous. No one was irreparably harmed. However, in our world each day what many people choose to focus upon leads them and others to suffering or even death. Life and God seem random, fickle, and even cruel. I wish I had a tidy answer for that. Even so, in the midst of our confusion, frustration, or befuddlement, we can learn to have faith in God's flow. We can trust in the divine current when we can't feel or comprehend him. Our faith can remain focused despite us asking tough questions and harboring doubts. Clarity and comfort come through a flowing faith - a faith in which our soul is laid open and laid back in God's current. Walking in mystery-laden directions, facing trials, confusion, and doubts, God's presence never ceases to saturate and surround us.

> **Tell me to what you pay attention and I will tell you who you are.**
> *Jose Ortega y Gasset*

disbelief, self-deprecation, and distraction

Disbelief, self-deprecation, and distraction are the three fundamental hindrances to deep focus. They thwart our focus and therefore our flow. They steal our experience of God's presence in our lives. We need to be ever aware of these hindrances and deal with them directly.

Disbelief keeps us stuck. Doubt is to be expected, but an outright unwillingness to consider another way will keep us stagnant, flowless. We may not believe our concentration upon God will unclog our faith. Maybe we have been living so long in the Sisyphus system, pushing our rock up the hill that we have given up on grace. We may ask ourselves, "How could focus upon God lead to transformation of any kind?" – *because attention leads to availability, and availability invites God's empowerment.* As we concentrate on God's presence in the moment as well as the activity at hand, we become open to his miraculous divine life moving in and through us.

At some point many believers in Galatia lost their faith in the power of grace. They were reengaging Sisyphian principles. Disbelief of this nature would keep them (and us) stuck. Paul communicates to the Galatians, who have been deceived by false teachers, that the only way to truly betray grace-living is to go back to law-living. We falsely believe that our betrayal of grace is limited to flagrant sinful behavior. But Paul says that in returning a rules-based lifestyle, the way of sin management, we fall away from grace. [128] Focusing fully upon God and his empowerment constitutes living in grace, real grace. And it's grace that leads us to godly, sensible, self-controlled living. The Scripture tells us that the living Christ lives for God the Father, and this living Christ now lives within us.[129] Grace works.

Living from the root of focus with God means working through our ongoing disbeliefs regarding our life in grace. If we have fallen victim to the rock pushing Sisyphus System, as we will sometimes, we need to stop pushing, sit down in the shade of our rock and rest. Maybe a nap is in order. Then, walk away from the rock, deeper into God's grace-filled flow.

As we learn to engage in concentrating upon God as way of life we will face setbacks. To focus upon God and our task in each moment proves to be quite challenging given the pace of our daily lives. It will require us to release any self-deprecation. Beating ourselves up is a waste of time. We have to embrace the fact that our concentration level will waver. Sometimes our minds and actions will be in the fleshly flow. When this happens, we admit it, thank God for his forgiveness, and re-enter the Spirit's flow. Time we spend berating ourselves about our lack of God-focus could be time spent flowing. If we blame ourselves and get caught in a downward spiral, a fruitless festival of un-focus will begin. Our freedom to flow with God includes freedom from condemnation.[130] God doesn't scold us, so it's absurd for us to scold ourselves. Rather than belittling ourselves, we can freely acknowledge whatever troubles us, and offer it to God as a way to move deeper into his flow.

Distraction also deflates deep concentration. It drags us from heaven and its perspective to a myriad of temporal places and perceptions. In today's culture, opportunity for distraction fills every minute. Our attention is a priceless commodity. As targets of marketers and the evil one, we are exposed to false messaging all day every day. As long as we live, we will face the opportunity to be distracted in practically every moment. Nonetheless, we are tasked with concentrating on a God and a kingdom not readily visible.

I have spent hours distracted from my intended tasks. Most of the time distraction leads to harmless activity. I may turn to watching television, surfing the Internet, thumbing through junk mail, calling a friend, reading a random magazine article, or even cleaning. Many times in the midst of my distraction I sense God calling me back to my task. Often, I roll through his stop signs. Finally, at some point I come to my senses. In that moment I'm tempted to harshly reproach myself, which only leads to panic or paralysis. My more mature response has been to take a deep breath, pray, and pick up from where I was sidetracked. As we grow in flow we learn to listen and respond to holy signs. When distractions present themselves, we acknowledge them, deal with them, make a turn, and move on. The Spirit leads, we follow, and onward we go, flowing together.

Maintaining concentration requires God's grace. It's all too easily for us to drift and sink. We can get lodged somewhere we don't want to be. We need God to continually rescue us from the abyss where disbelief, self-deprecation, and distraction trap us. We depend upon his grace to regularly retrieve us from these pitch-black frigid depths. He floats us upward to warmer water and into the sun's radiance.

presence: living in the here and now

The *autotelic* approach described in chapter two is another aspect of flow related to focus that connects with our Christian spirituality. In the context of our faith, the *autotelic* approach relates to simultaneously being fully attentive to God and our present activity. Writer Henri Nouwen called this living in the *here and now*.[131] Concentrating on self or anything outside of the moment will not allow us to experience sacred flow. Instead, we acknowledge and receive each moment as our most recent gift from God and surrender ourselves to it.

Many times when I'm with my kids eating dinner, wrestling, playing Wii, watching a movie, or playing outside, I intentionally inhale the moment. I savor it, look around in it, thank God, and let the moment wash over me. It's a sacred thing to really be with your kids…or anyone close to your heart. As we learn to flow in God's rhythm, absorbing the here and now becomes a way of being.

Christian mystics throughout the centuries have spoken to the importance of slowing or stopping to experience the presence of God in each moment. Evelyn Underhill asserted, "To be a mystic is to engage in the now, the eternal real, in the most complete way possible to man."[132] Saturating ourselves in the *here and now* is the place of God's grace. Breathe. Pay attention. Lift your eyes from this book and look around. Our great God, I AM, is a God of *now* – right *now*, with you, in you, through you. How many gifts have we missed as minutes, hours, days, months, even years have slid by without us really paying attention? Giving ourselves to each moment may seem exhausting, but this is how we embody God's restful empowering presence. Our attention and intention appropriates God's energy. Mindful God-ward attention in a moment allows God to energize us rather than the same moment draining on us.

> Highly productive and creative artists, entrepreneurs, statesmen, and scientists, tend to experience their jobs like our hunting ancestors did theirs – as completely integrated with the rest of their lives.
> *Mihaly Csikszentmihalyi*

More specifically, we attend to God for what he would have us do or say…or not do or say in each moment. As we concentrate and pour our attention into the moment, our path unfolds. God discloses what comes next and provides what is needed. In keeping with this, Francois Fenelon commented, "The present moment is your sole treasure for this is where the will of God is found."[133] God leads us to an *autotelic*, here and now personality in which we treasure every moment and live it mindfully.

The past and the future potentially serve as the enemy of the present. The past may haunt us in innumerable ways. It may stifle or paralyze us with the traumatic memories of past abuse or loss. Overwhelming ache from the past may numb our present, locking us inside ourselves. The past may torture or disillusion us with memories of long gone but hurtful failings.

Also, our past successes may haunt us in our present idleness or failure. Conversely, the past may also promote arrogance by regularly calling up proud memories of our former triumphs. We so trust ourselves and expect future success that we have no reverence for the present. No matter what our story, living in the past, brooding over it, locked into it, unable to digest it, doesn't allow us to truly embrace our here and now. Sacred flow only happens in the here and now. It's from the present that God takes us back to deal with our hurt, abuse, failure, guilt, shame, denial, and pride. He does so in the present with an eye on the future. God's present tense approach keeps us in his flow as we process our past, integrate it, and flow toward our future.

To the contrary, hurry and worry push us toward the future forcing us to sacrifice appreciation for the present. They keep us tied to the future and inhibit our experience of the here and now. Hurry and worry minimize or altogether prevent our focus on the present. They drag our concentration to the eternal *next*. Culture promotes and pushes for us to get to what's next as soon as possible. Regrettably, we multitask our way through life, truly experiencing very little. Life seems to force all of us to be jugglers, which eventually leads us to look like clowns.

A fundamental lie surrounds hurry. Hurry makes us valuable or desirable. Being busy equals significance. The more we hurry and accomplish the more we *are*. People who live slowly, soaking up the present are often perceived as underachievers, out of touch with reality, disengaged, or even ignorant.

More often than not, hurry serves as a coping rhythm to keep our mind occupied enough to stifle our worry. Slowing down means facing uncontrollable manifestations of our insecurities. We falsely believe that if we keep busy, our insecurity will disappear.

In one of my more recent slowdowns God confronted me with an insecurity of mine that lies beneath the surface stirring hurry, worry, and stress. God revealed to me that *I don't believe everything is going to be okay*. In other words, I don't trust God. In spite of my walking with him, flowing with him, and belief in his grace, I am still waiting, dreading the other shoe to fall. Life *will* fall apart; it's unavoidable. Buried in me as a response or outgrowth from my story is the dreadful belief that I am not going to make it. I'm going to fail at life. At best, I will be a mediocre second or third place, an honorable mention, a footnote. Even worse, I'm going to know horrific tragedy and never recover. Inevitably, I'm going to suffer, and when I do, God's presence will not be real enough to carry me through it. That was a

Faith is a refusal to panic.
Martyn Lloyd-Jones

harsh revelation for me to own. My intensity and hurry had been hiding it. You may be able to relate. I'm allowing God to massage that inner ache, trusting him to prove his presence and love despite where my future story takes me.

> *What I'm trying to do here is to get you to relax, to not be so preoccupied with 'getting', so you can respond to God's 'giving.' People who don't know God and the way he works fuss over these things, but you know both God and how he works. Steep your life in God-reality, God-initiative, God-provisions. Don't worry about missing out. You'll find all your everyday human concerns will be met. " Give your entire attention to what God is doing right now, and don't get worked up about what may or may not happen tomorrow. God will help you deal with whatever hard things come up when the time comes.*
> *Matthew 6: 30-34, The Message*

Jesus encourages us to focus on God in the here and now, releasing our compulsion to remain in the past and freeing us from hurrying and worrying our way into the future.[134] Our God knows what we need today and tomorrow and has the means to supply it. Jesus says there is enough to deal with today. In his kingdom we needn't waste a moment obsessing over the past or the future, we're meant to give our full attention to today.[135] The rest of the world does this naturally. We have been liberated to live worry-free in the divine current.

Seeking God's kingdom means seeking him in each moment, every day. We look intently for him, inside and out. We trust he will come through for us…even though we may not understand how or why he does so in the way he does so.[136] Sacred flow happens as we choose the present, the eternal now, over the past or future.

***

To flow is to focus. This root serves as flow's genesis. It's crucial that we fully give ourselves to God and whatever we are doing. Sacred flow's contexts are infinite. Living in God's flow we may find ourselves doing practically anything. We may be painting, doing relief work, sleeping, working a menial job, mourning, directing a band, surfing, laughing hysterically, babysitting, coaching little league, teaching, taking a walk, kissing, suffering with cancer, jogging, buying a couch, leading a company, skydiving, angry, attending a silent retreat, blissful, volunteering at a substance abuse center, eating a cheeseburger, or chopping wood. In the midst of these and other activities we will loose our focus. We will wrestle with disbelief, self-deprecation, and distraction. But we can trust that God will lovingly draw our attention back to him. We've been given the opportunity to flow into the here and now, whatever its content.

being formed by God's flow

1. Take a moment to reflect upon where your attention has been throughout the day. Write down what consumed you. Was it the present, past, or future? Ask God to keep you attentive to him and the moment at hand.
2. Ask God to root out and heal any crippling disbeliefs you harbor. Consider how those disbeliefs lead you to self-deprecation and distraction.
3. What distracts you the most? Ask God to redirect your attention when distraction presents itself.

7

Challenge

Living in the Spirit means that I trust the Holy Spirit to do
in me what I cannot do myself…It is not a case of trying
but of trusting; not of struggling but of resting in Him.
Watchman Nee

Resistance is good. Challenges compel us to grow. This may not be a welcomed ideal, but it proves true. Research has shown again and again that we need some level of strain to build our capacity. Maintaining a healthy body exemplifies this well. In order to significantly expand our physical capacity we need sound nutrition, regular brisk cardiovascular activity, and weight training. That's a lot of resistance, but it's worth it. Being fit prevents and reduces the risk of all kinds of disease and lengthens our life in general. Also, exercise serves our soul as a valid way to stave off or relieve stress and even depression.[137]

Very seldom can I remember exercising and later regretting it. There was that time that I went jogging immediately following lasagna for dinner. Big mistake, never do that. Other than that dreadful experience, I've always felt better about myself, and life in general after a challenging workout. Physical challenge is good for us. Typically, any physical challenge of reasonable intensity results in an overall sense of enjoyment. Despite the sense of enjoyment challenge brings, it's still difficult to initiate regularly.

We don't usually jump at challenge in all of its various forms. To do so feels counterintuitive. We seem to have an inordinate obsession with avoiding challenge, as if we instinctively sense danger. To the contrary, a small percentage of us are challenge junkies, the more extreme the challenge the better. These people find it difficult to turn down a good challenge. For some, their sense of self depends upon conquering every challenge.

Our body and soul need *balance.*

God has crafted us to face a certain level resistance or challenge. We need challenge to develop as people. Csikszentmihalyi discovered that for flow to occur, not only do we need to face challenge; we need to invite it, look for it, and dive into it. Doing so leads us to a more fulfilling life. Also, those of us who engage in a healthy amount of challenge enjoy life more than those who camp on the couch or those who undertake extreme challenges as an attempt to boost their sense of self. An optimum level of challenge leads to flow and personal growth. Most likely, the periods in your life when you've experienced the most growth were also times when you were sufficiently challenged. This 'optimum' level varies from person to person. Continually choosing challenges helps us find our flow.

> **God's love pervades us, flows through every molecule, vibrates every particle of our being.**
> *Gerald May*

Challenge is essential for sacred flow. This root has two distinct branches: clear goals and the challenge-skills balance. Both of these integrate well with our faith. In union with God, our clear goal is to walk by God's Spirit - which essentially means to love. Having been released from shame and guilt, we can welcome difficult challenges without fear. God guides the balance between our abilities and the challenges we face.

love God. love neighbor. love self.

Our dive into flow in chapter two taught us that goals provide clarity for our intention and attention. Odd as it may seem, this is true in our spirituality as well. Distraction may be kept at bay by maintaining focus on God-related goals. God births and accomplishes goals in and through us. Having clear goals sets our priorities and bolsters our focus. Goals lead us inward and onward.

Jesus' intention and attention had singular focus. Jesus was consumed with the 'goal' of doing the will of the Father. He was so consumed in fact that he was one with the Father. Jesus said his food was the will of the Father. He modeled to us the goal of kingdom living, which is doing the will of the Father. We are heirs of that kingdom, united with the King, and purposed with carrying out the will of the King.

Sacred flow leads us to live in, from, and for the will of the Father. The will of God for his followers is love. The pragmystic articulation of this goal is divinely empowered *love* – to love as he loves.[138] This is our goal by virtue of the fact that God *is* love.[139] Jesus expressed perfect love and he is our source, the substance of our sacred flow. He means to live through us, as us.[140] Love God and your neighbor as yourself with all that you are and possess. If we are to fully engage this challenge, this love-goal, we must wrestle with two significant questions *what does it mean to love?* and *who is my neighbor?*

As with the term *grace*, the word *love* has been worn out. Everyone owns it and uses it indiscriminately. It holds a vast range of meaning throughout global culture. The term is used to express the depth of Christ's passion in choosing to die for humanity, is spoken between dysfunctional family members, tossed about by professional clergy and by severely inebriated partygoers, "I love you man, really…" Despite abusive and other dismissive usages, love still maintains its super-natural value, especially when related to God and his kingdom.

From the Greek *agapao*, the term *agape* means to love deeply, divinely, and sacrificially in both a social and a moral sense.[141] It communicates the image of one who stands in wonder or amazement with her mouth wide open, gaping. This jaw-drop is our natural response when we catch a genuine glimpse of the extent and intensity of God's love. As we flow in this world wielding agape, we will cause wide wakes of jaw-drop. God means for his people to be known for a love that continually causes jaw-drop.

We hear one of the most full-bodied descriptions of jaw-dropping love at practically every wedding we attend. Unfortunately, this profoundly insightful description gets lost in wedding-world, its depth neglected.

> *Love is patient, love is kind, and is not jealous; love does*
> *not brag and is not arrogant, does not act unbecomingly;*
> *it does not seek its own, is not provoked, does not take into*
> *account a wrong suffered, does not rejoice in unrighteousness,*

> *but rejoices with the truth; bears all things, believes all*
> *things, hopes all things, endures all things. Love never fails.*
> 1 Corinthians 13: 4-8

Real love, deep love, God's love…and therefore God himself is patient, kind, *un*jealous, *un*braggadocios, humble, refined, unselfish, calm, forgiving, empathetic, justice-loving, tough, faithful, hopeful, *un*failing. This brand of love permeates us in Christ, meaning we too are all these things. We are meant to uniquely express God's agape in every circumstance. We are unique human manifestations of God's love.

Loving God, self, and others is interconnected and interdependent. The act of love is Trinitarian-like; one love, three distinct components. We cannot love others or ourselves without receiving God's love and loving God. We cannot fully release ourselves into God's love or loving others without a healthy love of ourselves. Lastly, we cannot love God or ourselves without truly loving others. All three loves interrelate with each being inspired by the other. In this way, God's love and our faith are circular and holistic.

> *The Lord our God is one Lord; and you shall love*
> *the Lord your God with all of your heart, and with*
> *all your soul, and with all your mind, and with all your*
> *strength. You shall love your neighbor as yourself.*
> Mark 12: 29-31

To love God means to live dependent upon him. It means we surrender all that we know of ourselves to God moment by moment, entrusting ourselves wholly to him. This brand of surrender breeds freedom. In our surrender-freedom we dream wildly and desire deeply. Our soul is ready for God's empowerment. As we offer every morsel of our soul to him, he tells us what to let go of and pick up in order to experience him more intimately. Without loving God deeply, our love for self and others gets twisted. We express a warped love through natural strength and questionable motives. An intense love for God offers perspective, divinity, and depth to our love for ourselves and others.

Loving God means we revel in and relish his love for us. We live without shame, loving confidently and creatively because are fully loved. God is loved when we fully receive his love. In receiving God's love, we are finally able to accept ourselves just as we *are*, and not for what we *might be* someday. Without accepting his acceptance, we essentially hold a higher standard for ourselves than God. We betray his grace by denying it. We get stuck in a cycle of self-hate that manifests itself in an untold number of ways. When we courageously accept God's acceptance of us, we become free to grow toward God, our authentic self, and toward others.

We cannot truly love others without first loving ourselves. Without healthy self-love our love for others becomes self-serving codependency. We love only in order to be loved. We please others so that they will be pleased with us. If we aren't confident in our grace-given inherent validation then we are constantly looking to subtly or overtly manipulate others to validate us. Personally, I have fallen prey to this more times than I care to recall. Lacking confidence in my value, I have gone fishing for validation from others.

To love ourselves in a healthy manner means we recognize God's validation of us. Therefore, we don't think too highly or lowly of ourselves. We don't allow others to trample us nor do we trample others. We embrace the sacredness of others and ourselves. We maintain proper self-esteem and self-care in light of our identity in Christ. This means we acknowledge ourselves as royal children, ambassador priests of God and humble human servants of God. We reverence ourselves as bearers and brandishers of the *Logos* of God, the most powerful creative energy in the universe.

> **A person connected with his desire will know whatever is critical to his success.**
> **W. Timothy Gallwey**

We are called to love our neighbors with jaw-dropping divine love. But who is our neighbor? A lawyer inquiring about eternal life asked Jesus this question. Jesus affirms that the way to experience life, real eternal life, is to passionately Love God and your neighbor as yourself. The man counters, "And who is my neighbor?" Jesus responds by telling the story of the Good Samaritan. The Samaritan, a half-breed outcast from the Jewish perspective, stops to rescue a half-dead man after religious leaders have passed by him. The Samaritan puts his journey on hold and uses all the resources at his disposal to care for the man. He offers up two days wage plus any additional money it takes to ensure the man is nursed back health.[142]

The Samaritan embodies what it means to love one's neighbor as one's self. Who is my neighbor? - anyone God puts in my path. The Greek word for neighbor, *plesion,* denotes anyone *near* or proximate. So, love anyone near you just as you love yourself. Love anyone in your path. Your neighbor is your *near*bor.

To love our neighbor means to advocate for them. Love is *advocacy.* Love advocates for the wellbeing of others. What we know as the *Golden Rule* embodies this advocacy – treat others as you would have them treat you. Advocate for others as you would for yourself, even more so. To love others means to live vulnerably with them rather than with a disposition of self-protection or self-worship. At its depth, loving means losing our life.[143] Jesus defined and modeled this sacrificial version of love, and we embody his life.

> **God is love. He is the ecstasy of Love, overflowing outside himself, enabling creatures to share in his life. Through his life they share the same overflowing force.**
> *Oliver Clement*

> *Do to others whatever you would like them to do to you. This is the essence of all that is taught in the law and the prophets.*
> *Matthew 7: 12*

Selfless love calls us to be loyal and tough. It's not for the faint of heart. We accept others unconditionally as we advocate, reconcile, and lend our voice on their behalf. Oftentimes this brings inconvenience and trouble into our lives. We stick with people and sometimes as a part of this we are called to stick it to them for their own wellbeing. To love others means to facilitate their reconciliation be it spiritual, emotional, or physical. To reconcile means to fully settle or resolve something. Loving our neighbor means helping them resolve whatever it is they need resolved.

Likewise, loving our neighbor means bearing their load with them. We willingly crawl under their pile with them, even if they deserve to be under the pile they're under. This pile carrying takes on many forms. Sometimes, being under the pile means jumping on top of it. Loving others can be complex and difficult. We sorely need God's guidance to lead us in how to do this well.

My friend Ty is dealing with a complex and difficult relational situation. His sister recently divorced. Brent, his brother-in-law, was repeatedly unfaithful to her. Though Ty fully supports his sister, nephews, and niece, he doesn't know how to "love" his ex-brother-in-law. His actions were more twisted than just infidelity. Prior to the divorce, Ty's dad bought something from Brent. He paid him twice its value in order to financially help their family. Brent kept the money for himself, and after the separation he stole the item back from Ty's dad. When he was caught and faced with going to jail, Brent offered to pay back the money but never admitted his wrongdoing. Mercifully, Ty's dad took back the money and dropped the charges. Ty still sees Brent around town. More than anything else he feels like swatting him with a bat. Not a very loving idea. How is Ty to love Brent? This is a tough one. He'll need to start by forgiving him. Many of us have to navigate difficult situations like this and much worse every day.

A few years back I spent a year working at a large corporation. Coming from a ministry background to a corporate setting, respect from my supervisors and many of my peers was not inherent or apparent. Naively, I worked without giving proper credence to corporate politics. I connected with most people on some level, but it wasn't clear whom I could really trust. Additionally, for most of the year, I worked under leadership that I perceived as coercive, manipulative, and incredibly difficult to follow…this perception was mutual among the many people in my department. Almost daily I had an opportunity to join in the slanderfest directed at the leadership. Sadly, I did at times I'm embarrassed to say. It was challenging for me stay neutral, much less to love or advocate in this setting. I stumbled, failing quite often, but I constantly had opportunity to move on humbly and creatively loving others in a tense, complex environment. Workplaces spanning the globe offer similar difficulties and opportunities.

In these situations and others like them, loving others can be tricky. We fulfill the *love-goal* in obvious and obscure ways, in direct and indirect ways. We may use kind words and gestures. We may be moved to stand up or stand down, speak up or shut up. The Spirit directs how we are to love in each moment. God, in his unpredictability, guides us through his uniqueness and ours to love authentically and creatively. The love of God has been poured out in us and now compels us. Our intuition, our gut sense, has been infused with God himself. The infinite Advocate lives embedded in our soul, serving as our purpose, method, and compulsion. We are meant to continually live and love by this Spirit.

With love as our predominant goal, we find company with the mystics, poets, painters, and writers…the artists. Love that embodies the divine is an art form. Referring again to Csikszentmihalyi's research, the artist sets and carries out goals intuitively. She is guided internally more so than externally. Love's expression is tangible, but its initiation is contextual and its method is flexible.

We ask ourselves each moment, *"Father, how would you have me love in this moment?"* As we trust the Spirit, we artfully love, employing an extensive array of activity or non-activity. Some tasks are quite simple, requiring only a moment of our time, while others stretch into many years. The Spirit supplies us the courage, tenacity, and divine empowerment needed to artfully accomplish our agape-goal.

A few months ago I was walking out of Lowe's home improvement store and I noticed two ladies walking out beside me rolling a cart with two bags of cement. I sensed God prompting me to ask if I could load it for them. So I did. No big deal, right? Maybe, maybe not. I will likely never know, but I know that I sensed God leading me to help. It took an ounce of courage to ask and ten seconds to load. Sometimes these very simple acts of loving kindness have a profound impact.

Love serves as more than our goal; it's our lifestyle. Dr. Csikszentmihalyi noted in his research that people who create, maintain, and concentrate upon a meaningful overarching purpose or goal experience flow as a way of life.[144] God's love, receiving it and offering it, serves as our overarching purpose allowing sacred flow to become our way of life.

living on the edge

Csikszentmihalyi established that to experience flow we must face challenges that roughly match our skills (the challenge-skills balance).[145] Those who consistently tackle challenges matching their skills flow through life. We need an optimal amount of resistance (spirit, soul, and body) to remain healthy, thrive, flow, and grow. Overwhelming challenges or suffering wound us. Too little challenge or resistance and we atrophy. Either way, our soul becomes sick. We're created to live on the edge with challenges that meet and expand our capacity. We're meant to live rhythmically, flowing out to push our potential and ebbing into rest and recovery.

Christ followers reach this challenge-skills balance by embracing the circumstantial challenges God lays before them and through self-imposed challenges. God causes and sustains all things. Given this, he arranges our circumstances, including the creation and maintenance of our challenge-skills balance. It's God who determined when, where, how, and to whom we would be born. It's God who directs our steps. The Psalmist reports that God has assigned our portion and our cup – our portion denoting our prosperity and our cup meaning our trials.[146] Our portion and cup provide us with opportunities to flow with God. He allows circumstances to tax our souls with his ultimate intention being to conform our character to that of Jesus. He knows the capacity of our faith and what is needed to move us along in his current.

> **O Christ, send down on me this Spirit with the Father, that he may sprinkle my soul with his dew and fill it with his royal gifts.**
> *Synesius of Cyrene*

Suffering in some form or another is to be expected if we are to experience sacred flow. Knowing this, the Apostle Paul encourages his readers to rejoice in the midst of trial. The dark night of the soul is a God-sponsored challenge leading us toward a more intense flow. I'm aware that this sounds a bit sadistic, uncaring, or out of touch. Yet these trials are not meant to test our strength, but our dependence. Challenges test our faith, particularly our willingness to trust in God's strength. God's expectation in the words of Jean-Pierre de Caussade is for us to "accept everything and let God act."[147] The freer we are from rebellious self-effort the faster we are moving toward encountering God.[148] God will continually challenge us, providing endless opportunities to exercise our depend-ability and experience his sacred flow.

We also strike the challenge-skills balance as we (led by the Spirit) initiate and undertake challenges. These challenges cause us to grow as we flow and flow as we grow. The perfect love of God that drives away fear releases us to risk. Security in our grace-given identity and God's acceptance of us frees us to engage challenges. We no longer have to hide or build and protect a superficial identity or reputation. Therefore, we challenge ourselves, not to seek validation but to live from the validation we already possess. Moving in God's love we readily invite challenge rather than dodge it.

The challenges we choose may be wild and beyond anything we imagined before we experienced sacred flow. Flow inspires us fully engage life, to intensely and creatively dabble, to bite off at least as much as we can chew and a little bit more. These self-induced challenges may require minutes, hours, days, weeks, months, or years. The challenges we choose will range from walking a mile to earning a PhD...from giving away an hour of our time a month to giving away most of our possessions.

I ran the Prague marathon in May 2001. I remember laboring over the decision to run or not to run. Training during the winter in the Czech Republic would not be pleasant and I hadn't run a marathon before. Upon praying and thinking through the decision I came to the realization that fear was holding me back ...not fear of freezing, but failure. I had never started something like this and later quit or outright failed. Prior to this I had finished an Olympic distance triathlon and a half marathon, but 26.2 miles was a different animal altogether.

I needed to embrace the freedom to risk (and possibly fail). No matter what happened it would not alter my identity or value as a person or as an athlete. Even if others thought less of me if I failed, it didn't matter. This security freed me to boldly challenge myself. I gave myself permission to quit or fail. Then, I started training. Ultimately, I enjoyed the challenge. I flowed through the first half of the marathon setting a new personal best. The second half proved to be quite different. At twenty-three miles my legs began to cramp. I finished the race, like a turtle in severe pain…but I finished.

When teaching people about living solely under God's grace rather than under Law, they often push back. They believe that if we live by grace in the sacred flow of the Spirit, we'll be lazy. Instead of choosing to challenge ourselves, we'll sit around (or sin) while the world fades to ruin. I remind them that God isn't lazy and therefore, by nature, neither are we. An insanely active creator-God lives in us, possesses us, and compels us. God's Spirit and our responsiveness lead us to attempt absurd challenges while tapped into God's indwelling strength. Challenges offer us opportunity to appropriate Christ's life in ours. We can live without fear, internally empowered by God's Spirit. Bravely engaging our circumstances along with choosing heroic challenges has become first-nature for us.

> **You have gifted me with power from yourself, eternal Father, and my understanding with your wisdom – such wisdom as is proper to your only-begotten Son; and the Holy Spirit, who proceeds from you and from your Son, has given me a will, and so I am able to love.**
> *Catherine of Siena*

***

If we desire to flow with God we must embrace challenge as a way of life. Goal-setting keeps challenge a priority in our lives. Since God *is* love, the goal of our life is to love as God loves. If we aren't loving, then we aren't living responsively to God. Agape-advocacy describes the nature of our love. The divine love we offer others looks different season to season, person to person, and situation to situation. But deep expressions of it almost always cause jaw-drop.

Challenge that flows keeps us on the edge – in the challenge-skills balance. Daily we are challenged to live deeply focused upon God and whatever the moment entails. We are challenged to be fully attentive and loving despite our circumstances. Since it's so easy to become disappointed, disaffected, and disengage, we sorely need to live into the third root, feedback. Feedback from the Spirit, our rhythm within, continually leads us back to the roots of focus and challenge and thereby sustains our sacred flow.

being formed by God's flow

1. Set some practical daily goals. Pour your focus into them one by one. Journal your thoughts and feelings about this experience.
2. Embrace love as your ultimate (and everyday) life goal, the rhythm of God. As you go through your day ask God, "Father, how would you have me love in this moment?" Then, ask God to empower your follow through.
3. Reframe your present circumstances as challenges and therefore God-given opportunities to flow. Consider what new challenges God may be stirring you to face.

8

Feedback

Abiding in Jesus is nothing but giving up
one's self to be ruled, taught, and led while
resting in the arms of Everlasting Love.
Andrew Murray

I started wrestling in as a response to peer pressure. Otherwise, there's no way as a husky seventh grader I would have donned a spandex suit and suffered public humiliation. When I won that first year, I did so largely due my physical strength and a few basic moves. Later, in high school I became one of the best wrestlers in Georgia. A primary reason for my success had to do with feedback I received and my ability to respond to it. In junior high I was too nervous and unfocused to listen and respond to coaching during my wrestling matches. In high school I learned to wrestle and listen to my coaches simultaneously. As I wrestled, I did my thing but also did as I was told. My coaches were wise, skilled wrestlers themselves, one a former World Cup contender. They constantly provided feedback during my matches and I wrestled accordingly. This led me to plenty of flow experiences and a lot of wins. Their input and my responsiveness were essential to my success.

Likewise, responding to feedback is vital for a healthy spiritual life. Being responsive sets the stage for us to flow continuously. Better than an external coach, we have the benefit of a divine inner coach. God's Spirit serves us from within and without. God's feedback is not always welcome or easy to detect and follow, but it's essential nonetheless.

embracing the rhythm within

A good GPS, global positioning system, makes getting lost (for long) difficult. Ever-orbiting satellites direct us wherever we desire to travel on the planet. If we get off track, they simply redraw from wherever we are at the moment. It doesn't matter how far we go or how long we betray the directions, the GPS redraws. We always have the option to turn toward our original destination or an alternate one that we choose on the fly.

God's Positioning Spirit serves a similar purpose within us. He constantly transmits signals, leading, guiding, and even empowering us along a sacred path. This Spirit is the path-keeper who continually reveals the *Path.* When we go off road, betraying the route, he redraws constantly sending signals for us to return to the *Way.* Despite where we go or how long we go off course, God draws us back.

> *I will guide you along the best pathway for*
> *your life. I will advise you and watch over you.*
> *Psalm 32:8*

Regular *draw-back* or feedback is needed to inspire and maintain our sacred flow. We need to remain open, pliable, and responsive to feedback in order to flow and continue flowing. As we continue our activity we may continually have to make adjustments in order continue to live from the roots. Our focus and challenges constantly fluctuate to some degree. Life is dynamic.

God offers feedback from many sources. The Spirit within sifts and interprets this feedback. We are meant to live attentive to God's *inner voice of love,* the holy whisper.[149] Sacred flow means for us to live according to the Spirit's rhythm within. We closely follow the Spirit's patterns, impressions, accents...we move to his beat.

God has given us what we need for life and godliness.[150] God has planted his rhythm within us. We have the Spirit-beat. Jesus told his close friends that he would send this Rhythm; the counselor, the helper, who would teach them the truth, the way in all things.[151] George Fox, the founder of Quakers, regularly directed people to be taught by this *inward* teacher.[152] We are meant to learn and live and move and have our being according to a divine inner rhythm.[153] Above all else, we know this rhythm to be love.

We live from every *word* that comes from the mouth of God. It's the living voice, God's utterance, the Logos, that gives us life.[154] We have been freed to trust God with where to go, how to go, what to do, not do, even what to say and not say.[155] The Spirit-wind blows and we move.[156] The indwelling Spirit interprets, inspires, teaches, counsels, and comforts us.[157]

> *The Spirit searches all things, even the deep things of God. For who among men knows the thoughts of a man except the man's spirit within him? In the same way no one knows the thoughts of God except the Spirit of God. We have not received the spirit of the world but the Spirit who is from God, that we may understand what God has freely given us.*
> 1 Corinthians 2: 10-12, NIV

With feedback, as with handling goals, we are artists. As noted earlier, Csikszentmihalyi found in his flow studies that artists needed to be intrinsically regulated when it came to feedback. Their intuition informed and guided the interpretation of their work and any needed adjustments. God's Spirit informs and guides our intuition. Jaw-dropping divinely empowered love serves as the standard. God gracefully leads us towards this from the inside out.

You've likely made some major decisions in life that felt almost entirely God-guided. Looking back, we can often see the fragility of the situation. We know God made the way by pulling the necessary strings. Irina's choice of college unfolded this way. Rather than narrowing her choice down to five or so schools and sending out applications, she applied to one local private university. She even turned down a scholarship to a local state school. To the contrary, her eventual school of choice was just starting a varsity program. To be accepted to this university was no small task as it annually ranks in the top twenty universities in the country. Additionally, the

> God is not silent. It is the nature of God to speak. The second person of the Holy Trinity is called "The Word."
> *A.W. Tozer*

cost of tuition was outrageously high. Irina had great grades and an impressive portfolio of extracurricular activities but her SAT scores were putrid and her family was not wealthy. Regardless, she sensed she would be accepted. She wasn't prophesying or prideful about it. In reality, Irina was wary of her intuition. She was accepted, attended, and graduated from her school of choice. When Irina looks back at that situation it humbles her. In her application process, she was working without a safety net. She intuitively sensed God's leading and he came through.

> **I believe in Christianity as I believe that the sun has risen. Not only because I see it, but because I see everything by it.**
>
> *C.S. Lewis*

Most certainly, every major decision of our life doesn't work out like Irina's college decision. We may have listened hard to God, moved the way we sensed were being led, and it turned out miserably. This doesn't necessarily mean we misheard or misinterpreted. It likely God was doing something beyond our vision and comprehension. We will not always listen or follow divine guidance nor will we always understand where the inner rhythm is taking us. Our part is to continually listen inwardly and outwardly for God's guidance and respond.

Having God's rhythm within doesn't negate our need for external feedback. In fact, it may intensify it. God may use anything to speak to us. Clearly, God uses the Scriptures as principal content. Unfortunately, the Scriptures have been the primary tool of those propagating the Sisyphus system. For many, the Bible has replaced God. Sunday after Sunday "should, ought to, and must" related to biblical principles add weight to the boulder we have been pushing. We often walk out of church gatherings with a heavier boulder and the encouragement to push harder.

In light of the New Covenant in Christ we may view biblical principles as expressions of God's love for us. Much of the New Testament includes behavioral or lifestyle instruction. This instruction needn't become a Christian code of conduct approached through the Sisyphus system. Taking an alternative approach, this instruction teaches us what it means for God to live in and through his beloved in daily life. Paul encourages the

Ephesians (and us) to live in a manner worthy of their calling. In other words, act in accordance with who you really are.

> *Therefore I, a prisoner for serving the Lord, beg you to*
> *lead a life worthy of your calling, for you have been*
> *called by God. Always be humble and gentle. Be patient*
> *with each other, making allowance for each other's faults*
> *because of your love. Make every effort to keep yourselves*
> *united in the Spirit, binding yourselves together with peace.*
> *For there is one body and one Spirit, just as you have*
> *been called to one glorious hope for the future. There is*
> *one Lord, one faith, one baptism, and one God and Father,*
> *who is over all and in all and living through all.*
> *Ephesians 4: 1-6, NLT*

Likewise, Paul implores, "Get rid of all bitterness, rage, anger, harsh words, and slander, as well as all types of evil behavior. Instead, be kind to each other, tenderhearted, forgiving one another, just as God through Christ has forgiven you." This is common sense instruction for those who are indwelt by Christ - who is love. For those who have been transformed, and are continually being transformed by God, it's only sensible to put evil behaviors away, be kind, and forgive. God leads and empowers us to do so.

We're meant to interpret biblical instruction as it relates to our identity in Christ and walking by the Spirit. This fits the paradigm of Christianity. Biblical instruction means to inspire a godly lifestyle that matches our godly identity. We're meant to read the Scriptures with the expectation that the Spirit will (re)teach us who we really are and the implications of that truth. God's Spirit provides us with inspired interpretation and empowered application.

God uses our community, our family, friends, mentors, etc. to provide feedback as well. So often, people closest to us make us aware of our blind spots. In these cases, their counsel is invaluable. Additionally, in life we frequently face complex problems. God encourages us to gather wise counsel in order to grow as people and solve complex problems. Our lives are so intertwined and interrelated with one others' that it only makes sense that God would use others to provide feedback. God meticulously weaves us into the lives of others as another way to include us in his work.

I often rant to my trusted friends or mentors about difficult decisions that I face. They listen patiently as I work through my thoughts and emotions. I want their feedback before I make any significant decisions related to my situation. As insider-outsiders they can offer valid insight. They are insiders in that they know me really well. We have a history together. They are outsiders in that they are not facing the same circumstances. We have a history apart. This puts them in a position to offer me meaningful God-inspired objective feedback. Over time I prayerfully consider their insight and go forward with my decisions.

> **Every spiritual being is, by nature, a temple of God, created to receive into itself the glory of God.**
>
> *Origen*

The rhythm within inspires broad discovery. Channels for new discovery may include formal and informal education. There is a wealth of knowledge to be gained from simply paying attention every day. We have access to more information than any other culture in the history of humanity. Living freely in sacred flow releases us to learn insatiably. Granted, some things we consume may give us indigestion and others may be down right dangerous. This needn't diminish our desire to taste new flavors. We need to explore. Through God's guidance we develop a sense of whether to swallow or spit out whatever we choose to taste.

rhythm and resonance

When I lived in Czech Republic some of my closest friends were a part of a jazz ensemble. In tiny pubs and cafés their piano player would bang away without restraint while my friend Pavel meticulously thumbed away on the base guitar, and the drummer blistered the snare drum. Out in front, Magdalena would sing reputable versions of international jazz favorites. I thoroughly enjoyed being in the room taking it all in, moving with the beat, and watching others get lost in the rhythm. I love jazz. The soulful music of Miles Davis, Ornette Coleman, John Coltrane, Dizzy Gillespie and the like often fill the background of my life. Some form of jazz goes well with whatever I am doing most of the time.

Given this love, Donald Miller's integration of jazz with Christian spirituality in his book *Blue Like Jazz: Nonreligious Thoughts on Christian Spirituality* naturally connected with me. Miller admits jazz is the closest thing he knows to Christian spirituality. Like God, jazz doesn't resolve.[158] By nature, Jazz, like authentic Christian spirituality is a free-form expression of the heart and soul. Many times, living by the Spirit's feedback doesn't resolve. It's doesn't provide us with clean-cut solutions. Jazz and Spirit-walking can't be graphed, charted, formulated, or mapped. Nonetheless, both are profound, real, evocative expressions of true humanity. Miller writes, "Everybody sings their song the way they feel it, everybody closes their eyes and lifts up their hands."[159]

Agreeing with Miller and taking these ideals deeper into jazz, there are several specific ways jazz connects with the Christian faith. More inroads can be cut when we consider jazz's loose structure, its narrative depth, and its cross-rhythmic and polyphonic harmonies. Jazz is a melodic train wreck, a beautiful mess. Jazz has inherently flexible un-inhibiting understructure open for creativity, innovation, and flow. Jazz artists use anything written as a diving board into their unique riffs and improvisations. They take what's in the box and craft new, distinctive sounds outside of the box. God releases us to live this way in sacred flow. Sacred flow's roots represent the "box" - be ever God-conscious and focused, live boldly, and be responsive to God's feedback. How these roots practically flow into our lives is our improvisational riff – a creative fusion between our uniqueness and God's leading.

Jazz has a larger narrative or story embedded with infinite mini-narratives. As Miller notes, jazz was born through African Americans recently freed from slavery.[160] Freedom supplied jazz's inspiration and essence. Like life in the Spirit, this free-form has significantly moved people and transformed lives despite its unwillingness to *resolve*. In some sense, jazz's story reflects Christianity's, encompassing freedom, vast diversity, innovation, community, creativity, suffering, triumph, joy, failure, loss, tolerance, intolerance, racism, mercy, and grace. Like God's story, jazz's big story fruitfully continues today and will continue indefinitely.

Phenomenal musicians along with their stories color jazz's history with more contributing to the mosaic in this generation. Within every performance each performer brings his individual story, his narrative, his rhythm and flow. No two jazz bands sound exactly the same (even if they play the same jazz standards) because the bands are comprised of different musicians possessing the same but different skills and instruments. They *feed* off of the beat and each other uniquely. Moreover, when the music opens up into solos, each musician expresses himself freely and uniquely in that moment. Every performance is a mini-narrative adding to jazz's meta-narrative.

In like manner, we bring our unique rhythm, our mini-narrative, into God's continuing rhythm. We respond to his Spirit as a part of the big story, the kingdom story. We play our instruments and play out our mini-story into God's ongoing gig. As a valued member of God's ensemble, we are invited to wildly riff and improvise within God's rhythm.

Altogether, jazz is polyrhythmic and polyphonic. The prefix *poly* means *many* or *much*. Polyrhythm or cross-rhythm occurs when at least two distinct rhythms are played simultaneously. The rhythms cross, overlap, often contrasting one another while creating a more textured overall sound. Each performer follows the parent rhythm and offers his distinct variation. Likewise, polyphonically, jazz produces more than one tone or voice, each with independent melody but all harmonizing. Jazz has diversity and unity, independent melody and harmony.

As each person responds to God's feedback in the community, they add unique voice and movement, creating greater resonance and texture in the holy rhythm. Living in the sacred flow we lend our individual voice and unique movement to God's and our brothers and sisters'. We create a free-form expression of God's love that comforts and inspires all those who hear.

Resonance creates depth and richness in jazz and music in general. Resonance occurs when the movement of one system affects another, *inducing* it to match its frequency. The second system echoes the first. The two vibrate in unison, resounding, creating a rich, intense, prolonged tone. We experience this when a voice or instrument sings out and another harmonizes or resonates with it. Together the voices or instruments intensify and the tone gets richer.

God desires for us to resonate with him. God's Spirit *induces* us from within to make this happen. His feedback leads us to move in unison with him and he works within us to birth desires and make them happen.[161] We get on his wavelength and echo Him. Our life echoes his with a robust meaningful tone. A system's resonant frequency is the frequency at which it moves at maximum potential. God stimulates us with an aim to conform us to our resonant frequency, our maximum potential. He creates the perfect rhythmic resonance and leads us to tune in. When we do, we echo the love of Jesus in extraordinary ways.

The opposite of resonance is dissonance. This mismatch of frequencies causes disagreeable sounds, discord, and cacophony. When we live according to the flesh (fleshly flow) rather than the Spirit, dissonance occurs. Fleshly living occurs when we deny God's feedback and march to a selfish self-created or culture-created rhythm. We lack resonance with God as we flail around looking for love in all the wrong places. In the fleshly flow, our life creates raucous unpleasant sounds as we attempt to master our own rhythm instead of giving our self to God's.

> **There is but one music in the world: and to it you contribute perpetually whether you will or no, your one little ditty of no tone.**
> *Evelyn Underhill*

Living in God's resonant rhythm means we match Jesus' cadence. We embody Galatians 5:25 – *keeping in rhythm with the Spirit in every area of our lives.* A lifestyle characterized by sacred flow is one of abiding in Christ, our deep-rooted indelible divine rhythm. Jesus declares, "I am the vine, you are the branches; he who abides in Me and I in him, he bears much fruit, for apart from Me you can do nothing."[162] To *abide* means to stay in a given state, place, relation or expectancy. It means to *remain, be present, dwell, tarry,* and *endure.*[163] Essentially, Jesus says hang with me, and hold on to me tightly. Stay responsive to my feedback. For your own sake stick here, catch my rhythm, and you will be amazed by what occurs. Frances de Sales calls this type of living - abiding in love and responding - 'spiritual agility.'[164] No matter what life throws at us, we are spiritual agile enough to hang on to Jesus. When God desires anything of us, we trust his life within us and respond in his strength. We continually tweak, bend, and stretch in order to live in tune with divine feedback.

Are we flexible enough to change our tune? Many of us don't experience resonance because our life is so loud that it practically drowns out God's feedback. We inadvertently tune out God's wavelength. Our soul is stirred with all kinds of dissonant or ambient noise. Hearing a holy whisper on the wind is difficult enough without added noise. We need to create a life less loud. This will require some tough choices on the level of breaking addictions we have to our favorite noisemakers. This may be internal or external noise. Daily Christianity consists of listening for and responding to God's Spirit. As a matter of assessing our spiritual agility, we may need to take a hard look at the dissonance in our life. God will lead us in doing whatever it takes to change our tune so that we echo his rich love.

> **The spirit of Christ, which is the immediate spring of grace in the heart, is all life, all power, all act.**
> *Jonathan Edwards*

***

Living from the roots of flow is the key to experiencing sacred flow. Living distracted by anything, even the fruits of flow, leaves us flowless. God's Spirit leads us to our roots and means to keep us there. It's from here that we move with focus, challenge, and become responsive to feedback. To close the chapter and this part of the book regarding living from the roots, I have summarized flow's roots in light of sacred flow.

Focus: Be ever mindful of God and the moment. Live in the *here and now* attuned to and empowered by God the Father, Son, and Spirit.

Challenge: Do the will of the Father; love as God loves. In every circumstance trust God to enable you to offer his jaw-dropping love. Through our circumstances, God provides challenges and therefore opportunities for us to flow. Led by the Spirit in freedom, we challenge ourselves.

Feedback: Listen and respond to the Spirit. Feedback comes from God internally and externally from anyone or anything God chooses.

Living from these roots discloses sacred flow as what writer David Augsburger calls a *tripolar* spirituality – *inwardly directed, upwardly compliant,* and *outwardly committed.*[165] All three components are essential to sacred flow's definition and expression. We direct our attention to our indwelling God. We comply with the Spirit. And we are committed to outwardly express his love. Going forward, chapter nine and ten outline sacred flow's characteristic fruits. These fruits enliven us inwardly and bring extraordinary results outwardly.

being formed by God's flow

1. Listen hard for God's feedback regarding the significant and seemingly insignificant decisions of your day. Write down what you sense God saying to you.
2. Ask God to broaden your perspective regarding feedback. Look and listen for God's feedback in places you haven't before.
3. Invite people you trust to provide you with honest feedback. Spend time alone with God integrating their feedback into your life as God directs.

9

The Inward Fruits

> For the love of God is always
> flowing into us with new gifts.
> *Jan van Ruusbroec*

The ball rocketed a mile high and deep down the right field line. I barely felt the impact of the ball on the bat. The ball floated over the fence, a grand slam. It was my third homerun in two days at our college's conference tournament. I looked into our dugout as I trotted to first base and shrugged with amazement. In the previous game I hit the longest homerun I had ever hit. It practically left the field before I left the batter's box. I was in the zone. I could do no wrong. I've experienced the bliss of flow many other times and not only in the context of sports. Flow is an unmistakable oasis whenever and wherever it occurs.

Once we've experienced flow, we easily become flow junkies. We want more. We even enjoy watching other people flow. They inspire us. This chapter and the next integrate flow's fruits with our lives. We will consider what happens when we flow in the divine current. What characterizes a life lived from the roots of sacred flow? What fruit does our sacred flow bear?

The fruits of sacred flow are many and therefore I have synthesized them and split them into two groups. I have distinguished the fruits by where they seem to have the most profound effect: internal or external, inward or outward. Some fruits have a greater effect on our inward life or experience while others more distinctly affect our outward life. To be clear, these groups aren't without overlap. The inward fruits affect the outward and vice versa. The inward fruits considered in this chapter are validation, identity, inner peace, control, and emotional balance while the outward fruits discussed in next chapter are unity, absorption, effortlessness, selflessness, and timelessness.

Before biting into the fruits, I want to offer some words of caution. It's difficult to avoid focusing upon flow's incredible fruit and our desire to experience it. The fruits of flow easily mesmerize us. The fruits amaze us whether we are admiring them in elite athletes or experiencing them ourselves. However, we can't manufacture the fruits of flow (or the Spirit). Fruit happens as a result of living from the roots of flow. It's tempting to put our focus on the fruits rather than the roots. It's easy to put the cart in front of the horse.

When we do so, we expect fruit out of season. We want full-bodied fruit year round without being fed by focus, challenge, and feedback. This is understandable given the state of our culture. We have instant everything, available all of the time. Companies work to provide everything (including fruit) year round, faster, cheaper, and in greater quantity. We expect instant success, instant fame, and instant service. So, it makes sense that we will be tempted expect flow's fruits without living from the roots.

This applies to our spiritual life as well. We may focus all our efforts upon *producing* the fruit of the Spirit rather than simply turning our focus to God. Only abiding in Christ in each moment makes way for the fruit of the Spirit and the fruits of sacred flow.[166] I'm sure it's happened to all of us. We were so bent on producing positive results or virtues that we got ahead of ourselves. We stopped giving full attention to God and the activity at hand. Our cart spun around in front of our horse.

All too often, we attempt to produce the fruit of the Spirit by using good biblical principles. We try life with great principles and programs meant to directly produce love, joy, peace, patience, kindness, goodness, faithfulness, gentleness, and self-control. The best we'll muster this way is plastic or wooden fruit. They may be masterful fakes, but fakes nonetheless. Straining for the fruits of flow instead of pouring focus into the roots only ensures a lack of flow. It's backwards, hypocrisy, fake flow, and futile. Our phony fruit often looks genuine but when tested or tasted the gig is up. Real fruit results from living from the roots.

Jesus declares that we can do absolutely nothing apart from him. He is the ultimate root. He's the vine and the Father is the gardener.[167] The vine and the gardener are the most crucial components; the branches are simply to abide or remain, acting as living 'flow-throughs.' Actual and spiritual fruit is not grunted out. Spiritual fruit comes by being surrendered and responsive to the vine and the master gardener. We posture ourselves as Spirit-conduits. Tapping into and staying attentive to the Source allows fruit to flow. We mature and bear much fruit by continually accepting the challenge to trust in the Vine, surrendering to the Vine completely...not by trying, grunting, or straining.

validation

Most of us are "do-*ers*" who sometimes "be." We are not comfortable as "be-*ers*" who "do." Culture teaches and incessantly pushes, pressures, and promotes validation through *doing*. This is the way of the world. Our identity and our activity continually fall short despite our level of accomplishment. We work for results, never quite feeling fulfilled or validated. We use all kinds of methods to dull the pain of feeling inadequate. Or we try our best to ignore these feelings. We continually strive, give up, or both. Subtly, we consume and perpetuate the lie spun in the garden to the first humans; your *doing* or *knowing* validates your *being*. Accepting this lie places us in a paradigm of endless and fruitless *doing* – the Sisyphus system - where validation eternally escapes us.

> **All our life is a celebration for us; we are convinced, in fact, that God is always everywhere. We sing while we work, we sing hymns while we sail, we pray while we carry out all life's other occupations.**
> *Clement of Alexandria*

In experiencing sacred flow, we catch glimpses of our true value. We embrace the fact that God validated us by simply creating us. We are valuable and validated as those created and loved by God. We are formed in God's image and carry his divine essence. While flowing in intimate relationship with God our validation becomes more evident, even palpable at times. God proves our value by living his life in and through ours. We experience our validation as we experience God. In God's flow, we experience connection with God and the sense that we're meant for something beyond ourselves.

God's validation frees us to live from the roots of flow without pressure. We no longer have to prove anything to anyone. We can withdraw from humanity's validation game. Having embraced our validation, we are free to focus upon God and whatever task is at hand. We focus, accept challenges, and respond to feedback knowing God values us immensely. In this way, sacred flow is self-validating despite any fruit that results. Nevertheless, when we live in the sacred flow, we not only experience the fruits of flow, we manifest the fruit of the Spirit.

identity

As it is with validation, discovering our unique identity is a basic human need. If we don't believe we are inherently unique, then we'll be motivated to carve out a distinct identity for ourselves. For many, this basic need fuels an endless quest for individuality in which we work tirelessly to create an identity. The recipe we use may include some combination of education, attitude, reputable job, trendy fashion, piercings, tattoos, music preference,

> **To be moved by the Spirit is an entirely new way of being in the world.**
> *Thomas Keating*

a particular spouse, a particular house in a particular neighborhood, or even a particular car. The list proves endless. Others have resigned themselves to a plain vanilla identity with little hope for uniqueness. They are left to agonize over or deny their ant-like sense of identity.

Being a healthy person and community member starts with understanding our god-given identity. Though we humans are very much alike, we also have uniqueness. No one on this planet shares the exact recipe that forms us. We are a result of divinity, DNA, and story. God inspired and enabled our formation starting a new human story interwoven with countless others. This divine recipe included who and when and where we would be. Sacred flow leads us to discover and live into who God intends us to be and what he desires we do.

> *Before I shaped you in the womb, I knew all about you.*
> *Before you saw the light of day I had holy plans for you.*
> *Jeremiah 1: 5, The Message*

After finishing a summer spiritual formation program in Czech Republic Roger was set to return to seminary as a second year student and assistant to the President. During that summer, God revealed a lot to Roger about his uniqueness. Roger soon grasped his freedom to flow and began to do so in an unexpected direction. Oddly enough, the desire of his heart was to work with wood. Roger returned from Prague and withdrew from seminary. His sacred flow had him pack up back in Atlanta and take an apprenticeship with a furniture maker in Southern California. There, he lived and learned, producing high-end furniture while a deeper dream evolved. Now, Roger the artist creates exceptional artwork.[168] A photograph of one of Roger's pieces serves as this book's cover.

Sacred flow led Roger and leads us into our grace-given uniqueness. Sometimes, as in Roger's case, this leads away from rather than into 'ministry' as a vocation. As we experience union with God, we flow into our authentic identity and related dreams.[169] In coming to recognize our true selves we let go of false selves. Flowing with God causes our true identity to germinate, fully blossom, and bear fruit.

> *You saw me before I was born. Every day of my*
> *life was recorded in your book. Every moment*
> *was laid out before a single day had passed.*
> *Psalm 139: 16*

inner peace

When's the last time experienced soul-storms? I've often described these soul-storms as *churnage*. Our soul churns in such a way that we can't experience peace no matter what. Our churnage may result in an overactive mind or outright physical pain. We may actually feel a rolling soul pain in our gut or throughout our body. Our soul feels like it's full of rotten fish tacos. We're deeply rattled, with no resolution in sight. Severe churnage dismantles us when we tragically and suddenly lose a loved one to death or a broken relationship. Or when we face life-altering decisions. Or when we endure suffering and persecution. A nauseating inner swirl tornados our peace.

Even now, as you read you may be facing a virtual lion's den of circumstances. Your churnage may be turning you inside out. You need peace. We all need an unshakable inner peace…right now and at all times. Sacred flow leads us into a God-given peace. Peace eventually comes as we surrender our focus to God and follow the feedback of the Spirit in the midst of our circumstances. Jesus offers his peace to his friends before going to the cross, "Peace I leave with you, my peace I give you." When he returns to them after his resurrection his first words are, "Peace be with you."[170] He has given us his peace. We possess the peace of God. We have the potential to experience a divine peace at times when it makes no sense to experience peace at all. God's flow calms our churnage. Like spiritual Alka-Seltzer, the Spirit of God mysteriously bubbles within, dissolving our churnage, producing divine peace within us. God promises, in his timing and way, he will settle us.

> *Don't worry about anything; instead, pray*
> *about everything. Tell God what you need, and*
> *thank him for all he has done. Then you will*
> *experience God's peace, which exceeds anything*
> *we can understand. His peace will guard your*
> *hearts and minds as you live in Christ Jesus.*
> *Philippians 4: 6, 7, NLT*

The term *joy* in the language of the New Testament, *chara*, means "calm delight."[171] Calm delight perfectly describes the peace that God delivers. Jesus says don't worry about anything. Tell me about it and offer your whole life to me, churnage included. Surrender to God and a peace, a rest, a calm delight beyond your expectation will pour over you.[172] Just be still, cease your striving and flow. Discover and know God as the living, indwelling God.[173] Listen for his voice saying to "you are my beloved, go in peace."[174]

A flowless spirituality leaves us to settle our churnage with do-it-yourselfer home remedies. This approach seldom works. Ironically, these remedies often cause more strain and pain. Whatever our strategy, it proves short-lived and limited to the natural realm. Sacred flow nurtures a profound supernatural peace that begins from within and works its way outward.

control

I've known Matthew since he was toddler. He's the nephew of one my closest childhood friends. Recently, Matthew spent five years in prison for dealing drugs. He was sucked into dealing by his need for cash and control. It started in high school. He learned to manipulate and control, pushing people and drugs. It paid off in material wealth and a sense of self worth. In college Matthew competed in wrestling while continuing his "sales" job. He was so driven that he continued to deal drugs even after someone riddled his car with bullets. Finally, the police caught Matthew. The state took control of him.

During his first two years in prison Matthew continued his manipulative ways, and as a result he spent untold hours in solitary confinement for his antics. After about three years in prison, Matthew softened. A combination of his awakening to the pain he had caused his family and friends and almost being stabbed to death turned him. Outside of prison, Sarah, a woman Matthew had been trafficking drugs with and later robbed, had surrendered her life to God. She had encountered God, forgiven Matthew, and began writing him about her new spiritual life. Matthew responded to Sarah and began to acknowledge God's

> **I was like a stone lying deep in mud, but he that is mighty lifted me up and placed me on top of the wall.**
>
> *Patrick of Ireland*

control over his situation. Over the next couple of years the two wrote often, sharing life with each other as they came to know God's flow and life within it. Matthew finished serving his time and was released.

Over a Waffle House breakfast Matthew shared with me his awe regarding God's sovereign control. Reflecting, he admitted his need for God to break him, particularly of his illusion of control. He concluded that he needed to be in prison all of the years he was there. Had he gotten out earlier he would likely be dead or back in prison for life. Additionally, he wouldn't have a reconciled relationship with Sarah. God's control broke Matthew's, rescued him, saved his life, and provided him with a bride. Matthew and Sarah now work together for a ministry serving those recently released from prison.

God's mercy and his sovereign flow somehow redeem even our poorest choices. As he did in Matthew's life, God mysteriously uses our most patent failures and the resultant consequences to draw us deeper into his flow. Absorbed in the sacred flow we recognize our circumstances as God-designed and God-directed. We sense God's control.

Often God's control annoys us. Francois Fenelon counsels, "Behind every annoying circumstance learn to see God governing all things."[175] We give ourselves to the flow of God's will not really knowing where it will take us, only that he keeps us in his divine current. Sacred flow leads us to embrace God's control and *self*-control. Self-guidance and restraint is the fruit of God's flowing Spirit. His Spirit enables us to flow in an orderly sensible fashion.[176] We maintain a measure of self-control inside his control. We realize his control and ours as we flow.

Outside of sacred flow, our lives are more erratic. Without acknowledging and embracing God's control, we are left to exact any control we can muster over our circumstances and our self. We often choose rule-keeping to assist us in gaining control only to discover that it makes things worse.[177] Our flowless lives career out of control, or by tapping as much will power as possible; we accomplish a tolerable semblance of control. Sacred flow illuminates God's control in our lives and our ability to rely upon his sovereign capability.

emotional balance

The worst trip I've ever taken started out well. I had spent the day with a friend traveling to central Bulgaria. This entailed a few hours on a plane and a few hours' drive winding through snowy Bulgarian mountains. But everything changed soon after our arrival. It was late evening and we had just sat down for tea after dinner when the phone rang. My wife was on the line. How did she get his number? This couldn't be good. Her voice trembling, she said our two year old daughter had just had a seizure and was in the hospital. When she last saw our daughter she was unconscious. She would call me back when she got more news. With that, the call ended.

I was in shock, numb. I was countries away from my distraught wife and my unconscious daughter, petrified and powerless. The earliest flight home was three hours away in Sofia, Bulgaria and at 2:00PM the next day. I shared the news with my friends in the apartment and we prayed. I surrendered the whole situation and myself to God as much as possible. God was in control for better or for worse. Needless to say, it was an excruciating night.

Remarkably, I woke with a surprising peace. My emotions rebounded. My surrender had effectively exhaled the situation to God. I boarded an early bus for the airport. I spent all day in the airport waiting for the flight. I was able to focus enough to read a book while waiting for the flight. The emotional saga continued when I arrived back in Prague. The doctors believed our daughter had epilepsy. Thankfully, it was later determined that their original diagnosis was incorrect. Sensing God's presence in the situation, my emotions remained reasonably balanced during this tumultuous situation and many others since.

> **If God can find a soul filled with a lively faith, He pours His grace into it in a torrent that, having found an open channel, gushes out exuberantly.**
> *Brother Lawrence*

Emotional imbalance can easily lead us to irrational action. We've all experienced this imbalance at some level in our work and home life. Our emotions got the best of us, driving us to say or do something regrettable. In more extreme cases people have been arrested or worse, sent to prison as a result of impulsive, emotion-driven behavior. Consequences of emotional imbalance range from simply being uncomfortable or embarrassed to outright lethal behavior.

In my flowless moments, I get flustered. My emotions get riled. I tend to get angry. I rant under my breath. More often than not, behind my anger is worry or outright fear. I use this snappy anger to cope or control my fear of being out of control, of failure, of inadequacy, or fill in the_____. In the situation above I was afraid my daughter would die or have brain damage. In my worst moments I was angry with God for letting this happen and angry with myself for not being present with my daughter and my wife when it did. I'm sure you too have your reasons for emotional outbursts or inbursts. Emotional imbalance is to be expected but it needn't be our norm.

Jesus points out that the flowless worry about everything. This is normal for those not tapped into the Source. Without experiencing intimacy with God we get bent and unbalanced easily. God's flow turns and returns our emotions to a healthy balance. Jesus directs us to consider the *un*worry of birds. Birds are so irresponsible. They do

> **People all over the world are withering because they are open to God only rarely. Every waking minute is not too much.**
>
> *Frank Laubach*

nothing of eternal value, fly about fearlessly, and yet God provides for them. We are infinitely more valuable than birds. God leads us out of worry into a proper emotional perspective and balance as we surrender to his flow.

Don't worry. Feel, but don't allow your emotions to get the best of you.[178] Live in reality and trust God. Sacred flow floats our emotions. As we flow in the divine current, we embrace our emotions and express them while holding tightly to God and his sovereign doing. We're meant to live fully engaged and emotionally balanced.

***

Sacred flow's inward fruits manifest as we remain connected to the roots. Fruits ebb and flow ripening in God-granted times and places. As we flow with God assorted inward fruits ripen along the way...in the midst of our idleness and activity, mourning and dancing, singing and sighing.

The inward fruits allow us to experience our true value and discover our authentic identity. They allow us to sense God's sovereign control. They breathe God's peace into us and bring balance to our emotions. This inward river of sacred flow's fruits finds its way outward.

being formed by God's flow

1. How have you tried to force (spiritual) fruit? How have you focused on performance or results rather than living from the roots?
2. Allow God to speak into the *flowless* places in your life. Invite God to unclog your faith, and flow into any dead places within you.
3. Journal about times when you've experienced the inward fruits of flow. Consider where your attention was vested when you yielded the fruits.

10

The Outward Fruits

We shall see Christ as the center and focal point
toward whom and from whom all things flow.
George Maloney

Many times throughout our lives we have benefited
from the fruit of someone else's flow. Flow moves us. In 1992,
Gatorade released a commercial that's still remembered almost
twenty years later. It was influential because it tapped into the
fruit of someone's flow. The commercial features basketball
great Michael Jordan. It consists of a grinning Michael Jordan, a
highlight reel, and a song, "Be like Mike." Remember? If not,
take a minute to youtube "Be like Mike." The lyrics went like
this, "I dream I move, I dream I grove, like Mike, if I could be
like Mike…" Why would we want to be like Mike? What is it we
want? We want grace in our action. We want to experience flow
and its fruits like Mike does.

When we see a flow-filled performance it inspires us.
We've seen them on sports fields and courts, at symphony hall,
jazz and rock concerts, in classrooms, at churches and in many
other contexts. The outward fruits of flow are evident and
contagious. We want to be as "tuned in" as the people we're
watching. They motivate us to flow and bear fruit.

We want to be like Jesus. We are attracted to the fruits of
Jesus' flow. Jesus' flow inspires. Like Jesus we want to live the in
the divine current of the Father and bear much fruit. We want
our lives to meaningfully influence and bless others. We have a
God-embedded desire to do so. Our spiritual genetics compel us.
Unfortunately, it's not as simple as drinking more Gatorade.

Only a life lived from the roots of sacred flow leads to both the inward and outward fruits of flow. The inward fruits of flow occur in conjunction with fruits that are more visible. In a sense, we may say that the inward fruits set the stage for the outward fruits. The outward fruits are fruits that more directly affect others. They are unity, absorption, effortlessness, selflessness, and timelessness.

unity

Stefan was traveling with his band to St. Petersburg, Russia during winter in the middle of the night. He knew that if they broke down or wrecked they would freeze to death before morning. They were traversing an ice-covered road in a small van surrounded by vast nothingness. The unthinkable happened; they spun off the road far into a field. The van came to rest buried in snow. It would take more than their small group to move it. There was little chance a single car would pass before dawn.

Stefan, crying, walked back to the road anyway. He stood on the road sniffling and smoking a cigarette, maybe his last. In desperation he muttered, *"God, if you are real please save us, send help. We will die without your help."* Stefan thought to himself that it would take many men to right their van. About ten minutes later Stefan saw a glimmer. It was headlights. As the vehicle approached, Stefan waved it down. It was a bus! The bus blew by and Stefan's heart sank. As he watched the bus in the distance it came to a stop. The ice was so treacherous that it had taken a kilometer for the bus to safely stop. The bus backed up and unbelievably, out of it piled a men's sports team. They moved Stefan's van back onto the road, saving the lives of Stefan and his band. Stefan became a believer in God that night. He encountered a God of unity, without limitation, who pulls stories together anywhere he chooses with perfect timing.

When flowing, we better perceive the connectedness of our world. We acknowledge all people and happenings as interrelated though we don't often understand how or see the depth of the connection. Our peripheral vision broadens to better observe God working all things together for good.[179] We become more mindful of God's sustaining presence in our everyday lives. In experiencing this unity we experience a glimpse of God's perspective, gaining more insight into God's insight. Our categories, biases, and judgments soften, and our love for others broadens.

This broader unity and our intimate union with God lead us to recognize all things as sacred. It breaks down the boundary between the secular and sacred. Secular vs. sacred and us vs. them merge once and for all. The sacred isn't just far-reaching. It's all-reaching. The miracle that occurred that winter night on a barren road in Russia didn't just give hope to an unbelieving Stefan and his band but also to the bus driver, the sports team, me…and now you. God's loving presence has consumed all things. This doesn't mean evil is not evil. But it means that God surrounds the god-resistant. All things dark are wrapped in light. Though evil has a presence here, the earth is God's as are all things in it. The sacred permeates the secular.

> How completely satisfying
> to turn from our limitations
> to a God who has none.
> *A.W. Tozer*

Without an awareness of unity, we live small, compartmentalized lives without perspective. We view moments, events, and people as independent rather than interdependent. We get stuck in ourselves and our small story. We view our doings or non-doings, failures or triumphs as defining us rather than being part of a larger narrative for ourselves and others. We separate the sacred and secular according to our finite determinations. Our stuck-ness limits our perspective of God's infinite grace-filled saturation of *all* things. In the divine current, we embrace a God from whom and to whom all things flow.

absorption

I recently saw a documentary about the famous French free climber Alain Robert, also known as "The Human Spider" or "The French Spider-Man." He has free-climbed the tallest buildings in the world - no ropes, no safety harness, no gloves…just spandex pants. In the show he talks about the freedom and flow he experiences while climbing. His legal freedom is intermittent as he often gets arrested following his skyscraper climbs. He talks about his focus. He says something to the effect that nothing gets me more focused on the activity at hand than life and death hanging in the balance. With every hand or foot placement he could fall. He becomes completely absorbed in the climb as if nothing else exists: his life depends on it.

Our spiritual life is a free climb dealing life or death. We make choices, hand and foot placements, which lead us to experience or not experience the divine current. Expressing how sin stunts our flow, Richard Rohr writes, "Sins are fixations that prevent the energy of life, God's love, from flowing freely."[180] We can get stuck on something lifeless and stationary rather than being carried away in the dynamic current of a living God. When we choose poorly we feel the absence and emptiness of sin. More often than not, the fallout from of our sin affects others. The Human Spider has a family to support. His death, resulting from and unfocused hand placement, would be tragic for them...not to mention him.

Robert has fallen several times, a few times from fifty feet or more, landing him in the hospital for long periods of time. He has broken his wrists, pelvis, various other bones, and suffered head trauma. Nevertheless, Robert's falls have not prevented his continued climbing and our falls should not prevent ours. The best way to be assured of secure hand and foot placements is not to worry and fret over each grab and step, but to be fully absorbed in God's presence and the task at hand.

> **Only wonder can comprehend his incomprehensible power.**
> *Maximus the Confessor*

The roots of sacred flow naturally facilitate absorption. A focused relationship with God in the here and now leads us to be absorbed in his current as we do whatever we do. When we are absorbed, our being seems to merge with our doing. Sacred flow affords us varying levels of this experience. Our mutual indwelling with Christ supports this idea. We have merged with God. We don't become God, but our doing can be his doing and his doing our doing.[181] Sometimes we experience this reality and other times we don't. Many of us haven't yet been open to this reality. Acknowledging our hands and feet as the hands and feet of Jesus, we may truly sense our connection with God and our activity. Any separation between us, those we serve, and God dissolves. In these miraculous moments we truly sense solidarity with God and others.

Our absorption benefits others. Those in relationship with us recognize our engagement or lack there of. It's noticeable to others when we dive into everything we do. This level of passion and attentiveness is rare and inspiring. Having given ourselves to God, we more readily give ourselves to others. We embody God's love, presence, and perspective. Absorption makes us good family, friends, and neighbors. Our full engagement positions us to love as God loves.

Without an open heart that dives into each moment, our experience seems detached, disjointed and dispiriting. We wrestle with a nagging disconnection between God, ourselves, and our activities. We half-heartedly pray without hope for absorption. Flowless, we limp along in the shallows of the river. We trudge along in knee-deep water, thirsty. All the while, God continually calls us into the depths.

effortlessness

I really enjoy movies. So much so, I once voiced to God an odd movie lover's prayer. I wanted to be cast in a film. God regularly uses movies to get through to me, so I wanted to be a part of a meaningful movie. The probability of this happening was minuscule at best. At the time, I was living in Prague, Czech Republic counseling and teaching and filling in for a pastor at a local church. After a church meeting one Sunday not long after my prayer, a movie producer sought me out and asked me if I could pray for his film. It was a short faith-oriented film in a dire financial situation. After praying, he invited people from the church to be extras in the film. Later in the week a few of us went to the set. I hit it off with the writer and director of the film. In doing so, I became an unofficial chaplain for the film. Eventually, I was asked to play a small part in the film. The film went on to win several awards and was nominated for an Oscar.[182]

This story is less about God answering strange prayers and more about grace-filled effortlessness. I flowed from voicing a desire to God, to praying for a faltering project, to being a part of an Oscar nominated movie. I didn't strain to be or do anything. I believe God flowed around, in, and through me to make this happen. I watched God create relationships and move me. I simply showed up and trusted God to do whatever he wanted with the situation. This odd experience really affirmed my faith in a God who makes all things possible.

Any striving or straining we do in sacred flow is straining in and through God's power.[183] We are to engage life and trust in God's effort. This is the meaning of perhaps the most popular sentence in Paul's letter to the Philippians, "I can do all things through (or *in*) him who strengthens (or *enables*) me." The term *en,* meaning through or in, denotes a fixed position in place, time, or state. Strengthen, the Greek term *endunamoo,* means to make strong, to empower, or facilitate.[184] Prior to this sentence Paul speaks of being content with much or nothing at all, when things are going well or miserably. We can handle anything life throws at us when we approach it from or in the state of the indwelling Christ making us strong, enabling, or facilitating us. This doesn't take away gut-wrenching challenge or suffering; it simply engages God's power to face it. Sacred flow makes our effort…less.

In his book, *Will and Spirit*: *A Contemplative Psychology,* Gerald May uses the terms *willfulness* and *willingness* to express two ways of living.[185] Willfully, we make things happen. We push, force, strain, and even manipulate. Ultimately, this is an exhausting way to live. It's not holistic or healthy. This earnest willfulness may seem noble at times but without God indwelling and empowering us it's strenuous and unsustainable.

On the other hand, willingness refers to a life in which we live open-handedly moving in God's current. We are willing participants with God in whom we live and flow and have our being. We fully engage God, our life, and our life with God. Our predominant effort is to consistently offer our whole selves to God in order for his effort to empower our every activity. We invite God's almighty power to work within us and through us.

> *Now to Him who is able to do far more abundantly beyond all that we ask or think, according to the power that works within us, to Him be the glory in the church and in Christ Jesus to all generations forever and ever. Amen.*
> *Ephesians 3: 20, 21*

selflessness

Teresa of Calcutta worked endlessly on behalf of the poorest of the poor in India. She was renowned for her selflessness. Her focus was Jesus and loving those he wished to love through her. She operated for decades touching the untouchable, comforting the dying without regard for her self. She simply didn't worry about what others thought of her, so much so that others were concerned about her lack of concern. For example, it is widely known that she rarely, if ever, turned away donors despite some having questionable integrity. Mother Teresa took donations from practically anyone, being only concerned for what the funds could do for the poor. Her unconditional acceptance of donations and people alarmed some 'reputable' donors and others who respected her. She followed the example of Jesus, who disappointed plenty of 'reputable' people by helping everyone and accepting questionable characters as his friends.

> I have found that there are three stages in every great work of God; first, it is impossible, then it is difficult, then it is done.
> **Hudson Taylor**

Additionally, Mother Teresa's personal letters exposed the significant doubt she wrestled with quite regularly. She admitted that she rarely truly experienced the presence of God. This makes her life all the more profound. With severe doubt to stall her selflessness, she continued to risk, serve, and give everything. She flowed *un*selfconsciously into the lives of those desperately in need and of no consequence to anyone else in the world.

Sacred flow leads us out of self-focus. It rescues us from self-aggrandizing narcissism and paralyzing introspection. It continually directs us to God's life in ours. We live by faith in his flow, not ours. His flow leads us to love as he loves - selflessly. When absorbed in this approach our focus stays on God and those we are serving, not ourselves. We don't waste time being concerned about our esteem, inadequacies, or pubic opinion. Nor do we put unwarranted faith in our self-sufficiency. As we surrender to the sacred flow our selfishness sinks as selflessness rises.

In a flowless lifestyle we think about ourselves so much so that we lose a realistic perception of God, others, and ourselves. While self-conscious we strive for God's acceptance and continued approval for our esteem's sake. We sacrifice our experience of divine life by attempting to save our natural one. We're unable to express our true selves or the love of God. We either think we are great, adequate, God's gift to humanity, or believe ourselves to be a rancid worm, an unworthy flea of a human, virtually invisible. Either way we're self-absorbed. Self-focus stifles the Spirit meant to flow through us to others. To the contrary, God-saturated focus leads to sacred flow and a selflessness that profoundly impacts others.

timelessness

Initially, the thought of a five-hour, ten-mile hike through a gorge seemed daunting to me. It would either be treacherous or boring. I needed it though. I needed some substantial personal time having been involved in intense ministry for an extended period. After all, I probably wouldn't get this opportunity again in my lifetime. I was on vacation on the Greek island of Crete. The Samaria National Park, housing a beautiful gorge leading down to the sea, was only short distance from my hotel. So, I strapped on my sandals and boarded a bus.

My trek began. Mysteriously, the five-hour hike meandering along the riverbed of the gorge seemed like one hour. It took me five hours but I felt as if time warped ahead and stood still simultaneously. I walked alone, but with many other people buzzing around. I didn't speak with anyone, focusing instead on absorbing anything God, through nature, would offer. Time sorted itself out again as the gorge delivered me into the quaint village of Agia Roumeli, teeming with tourists and the smell of Greek cuisine. The village stretched down to the Mediterranean Sea, an electric blue color so rich I can't even describe it. The beauty of the whole experience was moving. I experienced the timelessness of sacred flow. I was absorbed in the beauty of God's presence and his creation.

Surrendering to sacred flow entails not only giving ourselves to God's timing but also to his time orientation. As we flow with him, he bends our time to his will, at his will. God may speed time up, slow it, or both. Many times I wish God would warp-drive my times of pain and suffering and slow down my times of health and happiness. Unfortunately, all too often reality feels opposite. Nonetheless, God creatively uses timelessness as an imaginative instrument in our transformation.

Sacred flow leads us to trust God with our time, believing he'll make the most of it. This allows us to give time to others without feeling we need to hoard or hurry it. Living in the divine current means we move when we are moved. We learn to live into God's timing, his rhythm. He empowers us to listen and lean into our story and the stories of others. We savor each moment despite the pace of its passing.

When we're not living into God's flow we don't often experience these divine time warps. Instead, time weighs on us. It becomes an enemy rather than another of God's intimacy instruments. We may believe God has pulled us out of the game completely, sidelining us for a time. Or we feel he has stopped spending time with us. Or God is present but does little or nothing with our time, on our behalf.

Maybe the opposite occurs. God seems to be pushing us at a pace we cannot keep. We sense God's presence but time's velocity buries us. During these instances, time feels disoriented but not in the positive manner associated with sacred flow. Sacred flow resets our perception and time orientation, attuning it with God's timeless rhythm.

> Wherever you are on earth, so long as you remain on earth, 'the Lord is near, do not be anxious about anything.'
> *Anthony of Egypt*

peak performance

Research has demonstrated that flow leads to peak-performance and peak-experience. Acknowledging this, most performance coaches of elite performers hope to help their clients experience flow regularly. As spectators, when we see outlandish superhuman performances we often recognize the aura of flow. The performance seemed to reach beyond natural potential. It was dominant, fluid, effortless, and practically supernatural.

When the fruit of the Spirit and the fruit sacred flow occur through us voluminously, we call these "peak" moments. When God lives through us, it makes sense that we might accomplish extraordinary things. Our human capacity is maximized in the divine current. The long-term outward fruit of flow is life 'performed' beyond our potential.

Peak-performance is the ultimate expression of flow and sacred flow alike. But it also serves as their primary paradox. As I've stated again and again, we can't enter flow or continue flowing by focusing on results. This certainly proves true in our spirituality. We surrender to God with our focus on the roots not the fruits. Living daily from the roots leads us to flow then fruit; be it simply a more supernatural experience of the everyday or a seemingly impossible accomplishment. Ironically, sacred flow diametrically opposes experience-seeking and performance-based spirituality, but results in experiences and performances beyond our natural potential.

> **The Way that is Jesus Christ does not lead us out of real life. Rather, it fills this earthly life with transcendence.**
> *Michael L. Lindvall*

***

As we nurture the roots and live from them, looking inward and outward to God, fruit grows. The fruits of our flow affect us and others. In total, the fruits of sacred flow are not only the fruits of flow but the fruit of the Spirit as well. We manifest love, joy, peace, patience, kindness, goodness, faithfulness, gentleness, self-control as well as unity, validation, identity, emotional balance, absorption, inner peace, effortlessness, control, selflessness, timelessness, and peak performance.

When we live in God's sacred flow we get a glimpse of the big picture; how all things are interrelated. We recognize God as the God of everything. We discover each moment and its inherent value. We are able to accept our uniqueness as individuals. We sense deep intimacy with God and unified action with him. Our life slows and an inner peace exudes. Loving God, others, and ourselves happens more spontaneously and effortlessly. A sense of God's control pours over us. We drop any negative self-consciousness and fully engage the lives of others. Our emotions even out. We feel a healthy detachment from self-focus and the pull of the world around us. Time no longer rules our soul. Rivers of living water overflow. Our lives flow out into others' and they experience us as compassionate and contagious. We enjoy life despite our circumstances.

Having laid a down a foundation, established a framework, and sampled the fruits of sacred flow, it's time to consider how we can tap into this flow in our daily lives. The final Current of book called *Daily Faith in the Flow* will help us make sacred flow a practical reality. How do we posture ourselves to consistently experience sacred flow? Can we? What, if anything, can we *do* to create a fertile soul for sacred flow? Chapter eleven re-introduces the roots of flow as a soul posture, a daily disposition that nurtures sacred flow. Chapter twelve focuses on living into sacred flow and the hang-ups that might prevent us from doing so. A closing benediction sounds off one last call us for us to dive into the depths of the divine current. Finally, an appendix that describes spiritual practices is provided in order to help us stay connected with the roots of sacred flow.

being formed by God's flow

1. Which outward fruits of sacred flow do you see in your life? Take some time at the end of your day to reflect upon how your flow (or lack thereof) might have affected other people.
2. Ask God to redirect any of your choices that are hindering outward fruits.
3. Look for others whose ripened fruit is dropping into your life. Affirm them.

The Third Current

Daily Faith in the Flow

current: (adjective) - belonging to the present time, being in progress now.

11

Flow-Ready Faith

He is the source of the most delightful
disposition from which all goods of salvation flow.
Hildegard of Bingen

During childhood your mom and grandma, like mine,
likely pestered you about your posture. You probably heard, "Sit
up or straighten up" more times than you care to recall. This
annoying instruction was meant to help us establish habits that
would protect our long-term health. As kids, we couldn't care
less. However, as with most of their advice, this turned out to be
true and valuable. Daily life puts our posture to the test. Easily,
we slip or slump, crouch or lean. Gravity takes its toll on us.
Proper posture keeps our bodies functioning efficiently. Good
posture prevents problems with our back, neck, head, muscles,
nerves, and blood. It aligns our body, preventing pain, and
facilitates the efficient flow of our blood and other fluids.

Good posture promotes *flow*.

A flowing faith results from good soul posture. We can
consciously posture or position our soul with regard to
God...and everything else. This posturing of our interior attitude,
disposition, or approach radically influences our everyday
perspective and lifestyle. Sound interior posture leads us to a
healthy holistic integration and expression of our spirit, soul,
and body. Over forty years ago, Christian monk Thomas Merton
bemoaned that Western Christianity had lost its *interiority*.[186]
Promoting a meaningful soul posture as central and
indispensable re-prioritizes or re-*interiorizes* our Christian faith
for sacred flow. Graceful posturing creates space for alignment,
free bending, stretching, and growing. Good posture harnesses

the Spirit-wind who's current means to move us throughout our daily lives.

Three inner attitudes create an overall soul posture that allows for a full range of the Spirit's motion. They ready our faith for sacred flow. These poses that nurture sacred flow are not new or magic by any means. They are simply the roots of sacred flow engaged in the form of a disposition for everyday life. We easily slip into this posture as our way of life. Focus, challenge, and feedback can characterize the way we approach our day. *Find your focus. Choose your challenge. Follow your feedback.*

This posture fuses Christianity and flow, theology and practice, stability and fluidity. It keeps us pragmystic throughout each day. Finding our focus establishes, maintains, and recovers our attention so that challenge and feedback can be consistent realities. The way to consistent focus is *mind-setting*. Choosing our challenge keeps us engaged in life despite our circumstances. The way to continually face challenges is *rhythmic engagement*. Following our feedback results from an awakened spirit, soul, and body. The way to

> **It is not my ability, but my response to God's ability, that counts.**
> **Corrie ten Boom**

opening ourselves for feedback is *holistic awareness*. These postures create a full-bodied soul stance that encourages free movement and full engagement as the Spirit leads.

Let's briefly reconsider flow's roots that are being converted to flow-ready postures. God and the moment at hand serve as the subject of our focus. We're meant to fully engage God and each moment. Our ultimate goal or challenge is to love as God loves in every circumstance. Feedback comes from God's Spirit, the current within. The Spirit interprets God's voice speaking through an infinite number of sources. The Spirit initiates challenges, increases our capacity, empowers us, provides us with feedback, and brings our attention into the here and now. To *faithfully fully engage* summarizes the action that results when we live from the roots of sacred flow.

focus as mind-setting

For the mind set on flesh is death, but the
mind set on Spirit is life and peace.
Romans 8: 6

Keeping our mind set on anything for a considerable length of time is difficult to do, particularly in today's culture. Tragically, more often than not, if we aren't paralyzed we're distracted. Our distractions are boisterous and overwhelming while the voice of God speaks quietly within. We need to practice focus as a way of life. Setting our mind not only staves off distraction, but it moves us toward flow.

To effectively speak of mind-setting, providing basic definitions for the terms *set* and *mind* will be helpful. The term *mind* has numerous definitions and contexts. In our context we will consider the mind, "The totality of conscious and unconscious mental processes and activities."[187] Related specifically to soul posture, we will be speaking of the conscious mind. Primarily, this relates to our thinking and our thought processes, what we know and how we've come to know it.

The verb *set* in this context means to, "direct or settle resolutely."[188] So, to set our mind means to intentionally direct or completely settle our consciousness in a particular place on a particular thought or thoughts. On the whole, we don't let our thoughts run wild, flail about, or drift aimlessly. We maintain a particular mindset. We direct what we are thinking and how we are processing that which is happening all around us at any given moment.

Mind-setting easily relates to flow. Essentially, mind-setting is deep concentration or focus. It prevents what Csikszentmihalyi calls psychic entropy, a wandering unfocused mind. Instead, mind-setting is *negentropic* – leading our minds to order and depth.[189] Mind-setting moves us from simple awareness to concentration and onward toward absorption. Setting the mind keeps clear goals clear. It allows us to process and respond to feedback while still flowing.

As possessors of God's Spirit, we have the capacity to supernaturally set our minds. Paul explains to the Corinthians that they possess the mind of Christ.[190] The Greek word for mind used in this context, *nous*, breaks down the consciousness mentioned above to intellect, will, understanding, thought or feeling.[191] Our mind has been forever enmeshed with Christ's. Our mutual indwelling with God allows us access to some measure of God's perspective – his intellect, will, understanding, thought, or feeling. Unfortunately, I have met few people who have truly believed or appropriated this miraculous reality. Nonetheless, the Spirit continually leads us to engage and express the mind of Christ.

Being open and present to God and our surroundings brings a flood of thoughts and impressions. Mind-setting helps us process this onslaught of information in light of our goals. We set our conscious mind while our unconscious or subconscious mind remains subject to the Holy Spirit's setting and resetting. Speaking to the significance of mind-setting, Csikszentmihalyi writes, "Because optimal experience depends on the ability to control what happens in the consciousness moment by moment, each person has to achieve it on the basis of his own individual efforts and creativity."[192] Drawing upon the creativity and power of the God's Spirit, we sift and direct our mind, reigning in thoughts and thought patterns turning them over to God.[193]

Most of us have areas in our lives where mind-setting is a struggle. Nutrition is one of those areas for me. In my Italian-Deep South household, fried chicken was a side dish for lasagna. Our vegetables were breaded and fried or boiled to the consistency of baby food. Dessert wasn't cobbler or a cannoli; it was both! To make matters worse, I learned to use eating as a way to cope with any pain, boredom, or stress in my life. Overeating and eating poorly became a way of life for me. As a kid, it didn't matter as much since I was extremely active. As an adult it's become crucial for me to eat a healthy balanced diet, especially as I get older. I've discovered that setting my mind on *nutrition* isn't the solution. It's deeper than that. Keeping my mind set on nutrition isn't enough inspiration for me to consistently pass up second helpings. Finding my focus in this area means setting my mind on *love*. When overeating or poorly eating I'm failing to love myself, my family, and God in a worthy manner. I do everyone a disservice if I eat myself into state of poor health. In order change this pattern, I'm learning to set my mind on love and surrender to God's flow at every meal. You'll likely find that you lack love in those places where mind-setting is most difficult. Setting our mind on love means realizing a deeper love *from* God as well as *for* God, ourselves, others, and whatever activity is at hand.

> *Set your minds on things*
> *above, not on earthly things.*
> Colossians 3: 2

Love, the *clear goal* of Christian spirituality, is the sweet spot for our mind-setting. To love is our mindset. The mind set on love is set on God and vice versa. Within the context of love, our minds can be set on a variety of thoughts. In his letter to the Philippians, Paul encourages that the mind be set on heavenly ideals. He tells them to set their minds on what it true, noble, right, pure, lovely, admirable, and anything else that proves excellent or praiseworthy.[194] Our mind can move in countless directions within the context of God's love. Getting and keeping our mind set on love will take continual focus, patience, and grace.

> **A state of mind that sees God in everything is evidence of growth in grace and a thankful heart.**
> *Charles Finney*

Throughout life we have established rhythms of thought, emotion, and behavior that are both healthy and harmful. We formed these rhythms in response to our story. Our story includes how our parents, siblings, teachers, and peers treated us, our traumas, popular culture, and other influences. The patterns we've established go as deep as our brain chemistry. Our "set" patterns set our synapses. Setting our minds on something new or different literally changes our mind.[195] Christian spirituality leads us to the renewing or changing of our minds. Sacred flow (re)turns our minds to God and his love. Paul stresses, "Do not conform any longer to the pattern of this world, but be transformed by the renewing of your mind. Then you will be able to test and approve what God's will is—his good, pleasing and perfect will."[196]

This transformation allows us to flow more effectively in God's love. He continually transforms our minds as we surrender, focus, and cooperate with his grace. Most certainly, renewing our mind and continually setting it is an ongoing process that God's Spirit guides and empowers. Changing our minds, synapses included, takes time. This being the case, it's beneficial for us to establish daily rhythms that resonate with our mind-setting.

challenge as rhythmic engagement

I am the vine; you are the branches. If a man remains in me and I in him, he will bear much fruit; apart from me you can do nothing.
John 15: 5

Most of us have a stress addiction. We are engaged in intensive activity for long periods of time without substantive breaks. We have lived this way for so long that we are addicted to the associated stress. We are out of touch with any healthy fluid pattern of work and rest. Some studies have shown that it takes the typical person a few days of complete rest to break their stress addiction. If we actually take a legitimate week's vacation, the first three days of the vacation are spent winding down...just in time to start stressing about returning to work. We need to better regulate our diving in and pulling back. We need more ebb and flow, rhythmic engagement. We must learn when to challenge ourselves, when to rest, and when to repeat.

For God is creating us in the present moment, loving us into being, such that our very presence in the present moment is the manifested presence of God.

James Finley

Remember, rhythm is movement with a patterned recurrence at regular or irregular intervals. Rhythmic engagement consists of remaining cognizant of God's rhythm as he leads us into and out of activities. Living within God's rhythm is the only sane way for us to live. Remaining or abiding in him leads us to a regular flow-through of the Spirit. Jesus exemplified rhythmic engagement, demonstrating to us what it means to be a healthy human.

Mentioned earlier in chapter three, Jesus' life and ministry was rhythmic. Even his relationships had rhythm. He was guided by the rhythm of the Father. With regularity he ministered among the crowds, he walked with his friends, he attended parties, he visited with individuals, and he pulled away into solitude. He dove into the lives of others completely and pulled away completely. He rhythmically engaged in activity and rest, labor and leisure – all of which were a significant part of his ministry. Jesus engaged them rhythmically rather than religiously.

Challenge as rhythmic engagement inspires flow. Rhythmic engagement postures us for absorption despite our activity. We gracefully volley between intense challenges and we quiet restful times of recovery. Rhythmic engagement postures us to embrace a full range of challenges, activities, or non-activities, while remaining attuned to God.

Unfortunately, going and doing coupled with more going and doing characterizes our lives. Before long our going and doing becomes gone and done. Unless a more reflective and rhythmic strand of Christian spirituality is embraced, burnout and breakdown will overwhelm many Christians.[197] Regrettably, there is a popular notion, though unspoken, that any slowing, resting, or periodic stopping is unacceptable. As a result, many Christians are plagued by a sense of spiritual guilt. A lifestyle of ebb and flow equates to softness, slothfulness, or even heresy.

Ironically, the way to continually engage challenge is to enter God's rest. It's a posture of *rest* that makes way for our most passionate doing. Centered, dependent rest is the hallmark of sacred flow and spiritual maturity. Remember, Jesus invites everyone to rest and live freely and lightly under an easy, comfortable yoke. Admittedly, this seems to oppose rather than support *challenge* as an aspect of our soul posture. The *doing* we do is meant to be done in conjunction with God's strength. Rest in the context of sacred flow doesn't refer to idleness or passive spirituality. Rather, it reflects a quiet, proactive trust. Rest in terms of spiritual maturity relates to the New Covenant Sabbath rest described in the letter to the Hebrews.

Therefore, since the promise of entering his rest still stands, let us be careful that none of you be found to have fallen short of it…There remains, then, a Sabbath-rest for the people of God; for anyone who enters God's rest also rests from his own work, just as God did from his. Let us, therefore, make every effort to enter that rest, so that no one will fall by following their [Israelites] example of disobedience.
Hebrews 4: 1, 9-11, NIV

This is not a typical Sunday rest. The New Covenant in Christ is a covenant in which rest is our birthright. This is an all day, everyday rest. Rest becomes a faith-filled way of being and doing. The writer to the Hebrews entreats the readers to work diligently to take advantage of this rest. Don't miss it. Anything short of rest is short of faith and anything short of faith is sin.[198] Don't roam the wilderness of unfaithfulness and self-sufficiency like the Israelites. Enter God's rest. Drop any related shame, guilt, self-reliance, and enter God's rest. Divine rest will empower a life that continually but rhythmically chooses challenge.

All of our doing may be done from rest, with a restful heart acknowledging Christ as our life, strength, and peace. We are meant to work *from* a place of rest not *toward* a place of rest.[199] Approaching life apart from divine rest is an arrogant self-centered denial of God's grace and a declaration of independence.

A rest-oriented soul moves in rhythm with the God's Spirit. Rest doesn't restrict the challenges we face; it centers us internally so that we are better prepared to face challenges. Restfully, we courageously engage here, there, and everywhere. When praying, we pray with peace, when eating, we eat mindfully, when in conversation, we listen well and speak thoughtfully. In essence, rhythmic engagement as challenge has us trade restless religiosity for restful rhythm. Challenge and rest occur simultaneously as our way of life.

feedback as holistic awareness

Wake up from your sleep, Climb out of your coffins; Christ will show you the light.
Ephesians 5: 14, The Message

We not only suffer from stress addiction but from an ongoing hypnosis. The torrid pace of our culture can drive us into a zombie-like numbness that mummifies our spiritual life. Even worse, we stumble around in denial about our state. Oftentimes our awareness is primarily limited to our physical and materialistic appetites. Our spiritual appetite attempts to satisfy itself in programmatic church, is misdirected, or altogether suppressed. Unfortunately for many who attend a church, the experience barely jolts their soul. Likewise, those traveling outside of a spiritual community are rarely wakened by the fender-benders that occur while navigating life's highways and byways.

Living responsive to God's feedback means paying attention to everything inside and out. I call this holistic awareness. Holistic awareness is what writer Tony Campolo calls "hyperawareness."[200] Being hyperaware means being open, vulnerable, teachable, focused, and ready for feedback. It's a constant turning of our soul's eyes and ears to God while simultaneously giving full attention to our activities and surroundings.

This level of awareness or mindfulness facilitates a waking to internal and external stimuli not acknowledged before. We move from acknowledging (or not) the existence of our spirit, soul, and body to being reflectively conscious of our desires, needs, pains, and pleasures in these residencies. Also, we become more readily aware of the desires, needs, pains, and pleasures of those who surround us. Henri Nouwen writes, "It is by being awake to God in us that we can increasingly see God in the world around us."[201]

Cease from your own words, but in Power live. It breaks down rocks, mountains, old and sandy foundations...and makes up the Breach between God and man and breaks down that which made the breach.

George Fox

We open up and listen up from the inside outward and outside inward. God's Spirit speaks through practically anything. Holistic awareness heightens our internal and external acuity orienting us for open-focused, mindful, rhythmic activity. It opens us to God's feedback that informs and transforms of our spirit, soul, and body.

This feedback-ready posture wakes us from any fanciful illusions that soften, deflect, or pervert reality. Indifference and selective deafness serving as our soul's protective moat are bridged. Illusory or protective spirituality doesn't reflect Jesus' faith. Jesus faced his Father and reality with raw authenticity. A predominant theme in Jesus' life and ministry was living awake, holistically aware, and responsive to feedback. Attuning to God's feedback brings death to the *un*reality in our lives.[202] As Jesus approached the cross he called on his friends to be aware – to watch and pray. We are easily duped. Becoming unresponsive to God is an epidemic that has spanned the centuries. God calls on us to stay alert, listen, hear, see, and understand so that we can continually live from his feedback.

> *Watch and pray, that you do not enter into*
> *temptation, the spirit is willing but the flesh is weak.*
> *Matthew 26: 41*

The phrase 'living responsive to God' is another way of representing discipleship, or apprenticeship. We are learners. Holistic awareness awakens or reawakens us as spiritual learners. We constantly learn from God through various means as we posture ourselves to follow his feedback. We engage daily life as a willing learner. We also become *lifelong unlearners.*[203] Living in the sacred flow leads to the unlearning of former rhythms, religious and otherwise. Flowless rhythms and false concepts of God hinder our experience of sacred flow. A feedback-ready awareness means continually opening ourselves in order to learn and unlearn.

> *Therefore, I urge you, brothers, in view of God's mercy,*
> *to offer your bodies as living sacrifices, holy and*
> *pleasing to God – this is your spiritual act of worship.*
> *Romans 12: 1*

To be fully open is to be fully surrendered. Feedback as holistic awareness necessitates a 'wholly' offering. This *live* offering or surrendering of our soul reflects what Christian mystics call *kenosis*. Kenosis comes from the Greek *kenoo* meaning "to empty out." This verb is famously used to describe Jesus' surrendering of divine privilege before entering humanity.[204] To 'empty out' in the Christian context is to reject life in fleshly flow. We consciously choose to not *fill* ourselves with what the world has to offer. This reflects Jesus' call to deny ourselves daily and take up the cross.[205] We deny and die to any divergent self-paths. It's a brand of surrender exemplified in the "here I am Lord" of Abraham, the "may it be done to me according to your word" of Mary and the "yet not my will, but yours be done" of Jesus.[206] Kenotic surrender requires brokenness, humility, and vulnerability. We release any agenda beyond that of being holistically aware and moved by the divine current. In doing so, we become more our true selves rather than less.

> The only ultimate source of divine activity in all spiritual life is God Himself – "Christ in you, the hope of Glory."
>
> *Major Ian Thomas*

Being aware allows us to cooperate with God as he addresses our spirit, soul, and body needs. As we become more aware and attuned, we learn to distinguish and respond to our needs in a healthy fashion. God-empowered responses may lead us to specific spiritual practices, a nap, intense exercise, a slow walk in nature, family time, better time management, a silent retreat, intentional community, or wholesale lifestyle changes – i.e. quitting substance abuse, an abusive relationship, or an ill-fated career. We become much more cognizant of God's all-permeating presence, love, and guidance and therefore better postured for response.

Holistic awareness embodies feedback, and in a sense it encompasses all facets of a flow-facilitating soul posture. Being fully aware moves us toward focus. The only way to fully engage in an activity is to be holistically aware. Feedback as holistic awareness allows us to reflect upon the challenges we now face and will face in the future. Being receptive and surrendered, God guides us to and through these challenges according to his will and enabled by his strength. Additionally, awareness protects us from walking in flowless directions, taking on fruitless challenges. Finally, God uses our holistic awareness to root out fleshly flow and redirect us.

***

In life we are faced with an infinite number of situations, people, joys, pains, and problems. Life can easily twist our soul's posture into something that becomes unnaturally natural. Poor posture makes it difficult to initiate or sustain any sense of sacred flow. Posturing ourselves to flow is an ongoing process. This flow-readying of our faith starts by asking ourselves a simple question. *Am I living from the roots of sacred flow with a surrendered soul?*

Find your focus, choose your challenge, and follow your feedback. Let this sacred soul pose remind you that Christ is your life and he longs to live through you uniquely. Mindfully rid yourself of distractions and find your focus. Fully and rhythmically engage life by choosing your challenge. Wake up to God and follow his feedback. Be aware of God's loving presence.

With a flow-ready faith, we move into the final chapter. Chapter twelve considers what it means to live into the sacred flow as we live out imperfect lives. It will help us better understand and better deal with what blocks our flow.

being formed by God's flow

1. Take some time as you start your day to find your focus, choose your challenge(s), and follow your feedback.
2. As you go through your day be aware of what negatively affects your soul's posture.
3. When life gets you tangled, take a moment to stop, breath, and reset your soul posture.

12

Living Into the Sacred Flow

Our business is to love and delight ourselves in God.
Brother Lawrence

When I met Melonie she couldn't sit through a church service without leaving in shame. This was partly due to the religious culture at her church and partly due to her painful past. Despite her love for God, Melonie believed she was worthless, and unfit to exist in God's presence. She felt inherently inadequate and hopelessly lost. Any sense of rhythm and flow with God was gone and its return seemed out of the question. Christian religion and Melonie's shame had all but destroyed her. Amazingly, through our counseling time God re-introduced himself to her. He unveiled the reality of his intimate unconditional love. God peeled away Melonie's shame, and introduced her to a life with graceful flow. She traded religion for the Spirit's rhythm and her faith began to flow. Melonie's change was so immediate, drastic, and noticeable that a friend of mine who knew I was working with her called me to ask what had happened. She was experiencing sacred flow, and its fruit was evident.

Like Melonie, we all need to reflect upon our past in some measure in order to flow freely into our future. We need to root out the foundation of the flowless places in our lives. Dealing with these *stuckages* will allow sacred flow to become a reality in our everyday lives. By digging around in our story, this chapter helps us root out and dislodge the flowlessness in our life.

messages, beliefs, and behavior

Throughout our lives we have collected messages about God, ourselves, others, and practically everything else. Harmful false messages distort our sense of identity, relationships, and worldview. These damaging messages may come overtly or subtly, intentionally or unintentionally, from practically everything and everyone with whom we come in contact. To the contrary, God desires to speak his life-giving message into and through us. Life delivers plenty to cloud our sense of reality and prevent us from ever experiencing sacred flow. Tragic events, cultural pressure, daily distractions, the pain of our past, and worry about our future all have the potential to foil our flow.

How we interpret and integrate messages into our psyche and then our daily experience affects our flow. In order for us to re-pose toward a more flow-oriented disposition we must deal with our underlying false beliefs that have formed from years of message interpretation. This 'belief' work is vital because beliefs, rational or irrational, strongly influence our emotions and behavior.

Over time through various experiences, we form beliefs about everything from God to koosa (a Lebanese dish made from squash). Generally, our beliefs form through a recipe-like mixture of messages that we interpret and integrate. These message-born beliefs significantly shape us. We act upon many, if not most of them without a second thought.

Some beliefs aren't well formed or strongly held. For example, I may have never eaten koosa. In these cases, broader related beliefs that surface as preferences are called upon to shape our feelings and respondent behavior. I may not have tasted koosa, but I love Lebanese food and squash, so my thoughts, beliefs, emotions, and reaction are likely to be positive. This wouldn't be the case if I disliked squash or held a bias against all things Lebanese.

It's not difficult to see how our belief-behavior connection can hinder our sacred flow. Alina's story illustrates this well. Alina found it very difficult to be outdoors at night. The worse case would be riding the city transport at night. It panicked her to even think about it. She avoided shrubbery like the plague...yes, shrubbery. It sounds silly, but it's true. As a small girl Alina's parents warned her to be very careful about attackers lurching from behind bushes. These villains especially watch for women getting off of public transport at night. I doubt her parents intended to traumatize her. They just wanted her to be vigilant and safety-conscious. Nonetheless, this advice initiated an irrational belief in Alina's psyche that traumatized and trapped her for decades.

Our stories and our interpretive responses to them have created a dynamic belief matrix within us, a conceptual framework through which we perceive, think, emote, and act. Naturally, some of the beliefs making up our matrix are false, irrational, or overly skewed. These bent beliefs often torque our flow-ready soul posture or prevent it altogether, thereby inhibiting our sacred flow.

Since we ultimately live from our beliefs, what we've learned (or not learned) about God and our self is of crucial importance. Twisted thoughts and beliefs about God and our self establish twisted concepts of God and self. These two conceptions flow into one another to determine how we perceive and relate to God, ourselves, and others. False or irrational beliefs create a façade that we live into every day. In this case, we attempt to live in the flow of a God that doesn't really exist. We need to discover and embrace the truth about God and ourselves. This process is not about forming *perfect* or *right* beliefs, but about being open for God to love us, heal us, mold us, and move us toward wholeness and deeper flow.

> **The Christians life may be summed up as the consciousness that He lives within us, and we draw upon His infinite life in every situation we find ourselves in.**
> *Malcolm Smith*

One of my favorite films is *The Matrix*, the first in the trilogy. Ten years and thirty or so viewings later, the film still inspires me. It stirs me because it's an expression of our journey toward wholeness. I've never interpreted the main character *Neo* as a messiah-like figure. I've always interpreted him as you and me. Mr. Anderson, a normal everyday person and a rebel, sleeplessly searches and longs for something more, something real. He seeks the truth and a mysterious, said to be dangerous, god-like person, Morpheus. Mr. Anderson is flushed from the matrix, reborn, redeemed from being no one to being *the One*. He transforms from *old* man to *new* man – Neo. He goes from death to life, from disillusioned to enlightened, from a predetermined meaningless destiny to a destiny that means something to all of humanity. Neo finds *real* life early in the film and spends the rest of the film 'working out his salvation.' He must live into his true identity – what it means to be *the One*. We find ourselves in the same situation. We are the sought after *One*, discovering what it means to be fully flowing in reality as a person of divine destiny.

Moving out of our warped belief *matrix* towards wholeness with regard to our conception of God and our self, means moving out of denial and idolatry. Denial keeps us trapped in our matrix. We can't experience God's flow if we can't admit our need, pain, false belief, or lack of rhythm. As we move out of denial, we shed the crust and rust on our soul and begin to consider another way, reality. Reality can seem difficult, even overwhelming to us (as it did to Neo initially). Thankfully, we can face it within God's flow drawing upon his guidance and strength.

Idolatry literally and figuratively means *image worship*.[207] To be idolatrous means we worship *images* that do not match God-reality. We worship perverted images of God or material things as God. At best, we create holograms of the true God. Generally, we conjure up a personified male God who is squishy and agreeable or tyrannical, aggressive, and intolerant. He is an unholy collage that bounds a boundless God and perverts divine love. God becomes who we want or need God to be, for better or for worse. As Dietrich Bonhoeffer wrote, "To everyone God is the kind of God he believes in."[208] Sacred flow means to awaken us to a new image of God, one we allow God to create. As we live into the sacred flow God reshapes our perspective of him and ourselves.

> **God, to be God, must transcend what is. He must be the maker of what ought to be.**
> *Rufus M. Jones*

Ask God to walk you through your images and beliefs about him including how and when they formed. You might be surprised to discover how much was formed by what your parents did or did not do, by their presence or lack thereof. Take the time to prayerfully dig.

Patrick's concept of God directly reflected how he perceived his earthly father. Patrick's dad, Rory, was a loyal provider for the family. Undoubtedly, Rory loved his family but he also had a short fuse with them. Rory revered God to the point of blurring the line between reverence and an unhealthy fear. With this modeling, Patrick saw God as a loving, somewhat distant dictator-like Father to be revered, respected, and never crossed. Patrick loved his despot God and his despot God loved him. God's demands and expectations were more unwritten than written. God's love and presence felt performance-based and precarious. In response, Patrick, longing for love, performed and performed more. His young adult life became about measuring up, being the best soldier-son he could be. Though Patrick worked tirelessly to please Rory and God, he always felt inadequate. Patrick's beliefs and behavior make sense given his story, and it's likely yours do as well.

Ask God to walk you through your beliefs about church and spirituality and how they were formed. Our childhood, inside or outside of organized religion, has affected the way we perceive church and spirituality. What we were taught about God at a young age shapes our concept of God, church, and spirituality. A couple of stories best illustrate this.

A friend of mine was haunted as a child by a song she heard in Sunday school. It goes something like this, "Be careful little eyes what you see, the Father's up above, and he's looking down in love, be careful little eyes what you see...be careful little hands what you touch..." You get the idea. She gleaned that God is up there looking down at us and it doesn't feel like it's in love. He is watching and waiting for us to make a mistake. Be careful. Be good. Be perfect...or else.

With all the children huddled around him at the front of the sanctuary, the pastor started his children's sermon by telling the kids about Jesus' sacrifice for them. Then, using grapes to represent people, he loaded a blender. He explained that many grapes would not choose to believe in Jesus. The grapes in the blender represented those unbelieving people. He went on to say that at the end of time those who didn't believe would be destroyed. Then, he cranked the blender. I heard this story over ten years ago and I'm still bothered by its dreadful, traumatic content. I can only imagine what a seven-year-old gleaned from this vivid "biblical" illustration.

Life has dealt many of us messages that have led to poor self-concepts. If we're not self-loathing, we're somewhere between arrogance and narcissism. Either way, we're not loving or even liking ourselves well. Many who have struggled through abusive or otherwise difficult childhoods don't recognize how dramatically this has affected their self-concept. Others have come away with skewed beliefs about themselves despite a positive upbringing guided by caring parents. Still others suffer from recent traumas that have pummeled their sense of self. Pain from our ancient or recent past carries enough weight to distort our healthy soul posture and sink our sacred flow. As with our God concept, we can ask God to walk us through our story in order to unearth any self-concept crushers.

Enmeshed with whatever our beliefs are about our self is a single God-established core need. This need and what we believe about its fulfillment strongly informs our concept of self. We all need *love*. Love encompasses other basic needs like *acceptance, value, identity, and security* or *peace*. Genuine love requires acceptance. Love acknowledges and affirms identity and value. Love naturally desires to protect, preserve, and secure. This inherent need for love tightly relates with our concept of self.

When I met Tony he was completely finished with God. He had served as a pastor and a missionary for years and now he sat with me for intensive counseling. To be honest, I did not expect much, if anything, to happen during our short fifteen days. He was raw with lifelong pain, feeling unloved and unlovable. He was experiencing a rocky relationship with God, his father, and his ministry. Tony's primary way to cope with life had been ministry. Doing ministry granted him love in the form of value, acceptance, identity, and security. Increasingly, he felt he couldn't measure up to God's expectations, his father's, his congregation's, or his own. He had been emotionally beat up by each. He had given his all and it wasn't enough. Not only was God distant, he was disappointed. With this bubbling up from his belief system, Tony was broken, depressed, hopeless, and angry. He believed no one could love him, including himself.

We talked through the origin of many of his false or irrational beliefs about God, ministry, himself, and others. We sifted his story, how it played out, and how he interpreted it to form a diseased belief matrix. I helped him see how his beliefs led to his current soul posture and coping rhythms. Tony needed an extreme belief makeover. He started by engaging new ideas about a graceful God who cherished and loved him for him, not his performance. This sparked wholesale restoration in his thoughts and his beliefs about God, ministry, himself, and others. As Tony began to recognize God, himself, and others as lovable and loved his soul revived. His faith started to flow.

To be healthy and whole people we need to know that we are lovable and loved. When we believe this core need is not being met, we seek resolution ravenously, doing so consciously and subconsciously. We medicate with practically anything or anyone that we think will make us feel good, loved, and lovable. The cost and consequence of this variety of medication is staggering.

The medication we use to deal with our longings can also be understood as coping rhythms. These are particular behaviors we *use* in an attempt to get our needs met. Even though we receive God's love and live in it we will still engage coping rhythms. Particularly under stress we resort to coping rather than trusting in God's love to meet our needs. In order to live into the sacred flow we need to unearth and address our coping rhythms.

I'm rarely shocked when people share how they've coped with the pain in their life. We will do anything for love. Our coping rhythms can be boring, innovative, or horrific. Some are mild and others are malevolent. Some look sharp while others look sheepish. We do wildly creative activities in an attempt to get our needs met. We construct elaborate false identities to feel okay about ourselves. We meticulously cheat people to become wealthy thereby fulfilling our need for significance and security. We

> **Our true self needs neither a muted trumpet to herald our arrival nor a gaudy soapbox to rivet attention from others. We give glory to God simply by being ourselves.**
> *Brennan Manning*

develop a remarkable wit, gathering laughter as value. Darker rhythms may include abusing others or ourselves emotionally, physically, or sexually to gain a sense of control or validation. Conversely, we hide or withdraw in numerous ways feeling unworthy of love. There is no limit to the avenues we choose in a vain effort to prop up our self-concept and satisfy our God-embedded love-need. All these charades hinder our opportunity to experience sacred flow.

More often than not, we over-do or pervert a healthy concept of self and related rhythms. For example, eating is healthy; overeating is not, even if I am gorging on steamed broccoli (not likely). Having a great sense of humor is a gift. Using this gift to secure significance is not. Working hard is healthy and honorable. Becoming a workaholic in order to have self-worth is not. Net worth doesn't equal self-worth. Loving others is healthy. Needing or obsessing over their love hoping it will validate us is not. Celebration is healthy. Substance abuse while partying in order to escape reality is not. This list could continue indefinitely. The definition of compulsively overdoing anything is called *addiction*. Many of our distortions of self and coping rhythms are nothing short of addiction.

> **Be patient with everyone, but above all with yourself.**
> *Francis de Sales*

Fortunately, through the power and beauty of the gospel of grace, God meets our core need. God declares us his *beloved* children – lovable and loved.[209] Divine love has the power to break our addictions and make us whole. As a people becoming whole, we flow with God and learn to accept ourselves as lovable, worthy, and secure in God's sovereignty. Living from this place of fulfillment, we are free to move beyond voracious need-meeting. Living into the sacred flow means letting go of our coping rhythms and living *into* and *from* God's love for us.

Healing our concepts of God and self as well as dealing with the guilt associated with ongoing fleshly coping rhythms requires forgiveness. We're not totally free until we forgive. Essentially, to forgive is to release a debt. A person who has offended us has created a debt; they owe us. To forgive them means releasing them from whatever they owe us. It means releasing them without condition or repayment. Releasing others releases *us*. Without forgiveness we carry everyone and everything that has ever hurt us. This weight certainly torques our soul's posture. Instead of flowing, we sulk, sink, bend, crack, and eventually break.

Many of us may feel God owes us. He allowed harsh circumstances in our life or surrounded us with harsh people. God took someone dear to us unexpectedly. God simply hasn't come through for us. We need to forgive God for his unwillingness to meet our expectations. Of course God doesn't need us to forgive him. We can't see the eternal picture. So, we are left with the tension of faith and mystery, trusting that God has been with us through it all, and is working everything in our story together for good. To freely flow, we'll have to forgive God.

Likewise, we must forgive others to set ourselves free. Forgiving others is not predicated upon their asking. This small detail makes forgiveness excruciatingly painful when we need to forgive people who deny they've offended us or simply refuse to ask for forgiveness. Others may not even know they've hurt us. Genuine forgiveness requires grace. We intentionally choose to forgive, trusting God's grace in his timing to heal our associated emotional wounds. Our releasing them doesn't necessarily equate to forgetting their offense or immediate emotional release for us. Forgiveness may seem unimaginable or just impractical, but it's essential for healthy spirituality.

Never underestimate the power of forgiveness. Profound change in people occurs when they choose to grant forgiveness to others. Through the grace of God many have courageously forgiven those responsible for severely wounding them. For both nominal and horrific offenses they've released moms, dads, brothers, sisters, grandmas, grandpas, uncles, aunts, cousins, friends, foes, strangers, pastors, second grade teachers, Sunday school leaders, etc. Most significantly though, they forgave themselves. They offloaded the condemnation they had piled on themselves over the years. They dropped their self-hatred. They turned to love their enemy, themselves.

Healing our concepts of God and self, including the choice to continually forgive, ready and steady us for sacred flow. They remove the weight from our soul that prevents a flow-ready posture. We must befriend our story in all its glory, trauma, and tragedy. Via the Spirit's guidance and illumination, while flowing we contemplate our beliefs about God, ourselves, and others, receive God's love, love in return, and forgive. All this being said, I recognize that our belief matrix and forgiveness issues are complex. In the midst of our twisted complex issues, we trust God, the divine current within and without, to bring wholeness.

the good, the bad, and the ugly

Because sacred flow depends upon the divine current rather than a current we create, experiencing flow is possible through the good, the bad, and the ugly in our lives. Were it human-generated, sacred flow would only occur on our best days. In other words, if our circumstances are positive and we perform well, then we flow. If they are negative and we don't perform well, then we fail God and lack his flow. This betrays the nature of God and flow. We exist in the divine current whether we acknowledge it or not. God's flow abides and we have the opportunity to abide in it.

Our flow-ready posture keeps us connected with flow's roots through life's good, bad, and ugly. Finding focus, engaging challenges, and responding to the Spirit's feedback nurture flow under the harshest conditions. God has not promised circumstances free of pain, anguish, suffering, or want. God promises his acceptance, presence, and flow despite what occurs. As we navigate life's peaks and valleys we may be faced with maintaining a flow fertile soul posture under exceptionally difficult circumstances.

Good, bad, and ugly circumstances greatly influence our emotions. If we are to flow through these situations we will need to embrace our emotions no matter how dark, confusing, or embarrassing they may be. Peter Scazzero articulately submits, "Emotional health powerfully anchors me in the love of God by affirming that I am worthy of feeling, worthy of being alive, and lovable even when I am brutally honest about the good, the bad, and the ugly deep beneath the surface of my iceberg."[210] We need not fear our emotions despite their intensity. Repressing emotions keeps our soul clogged and stunts our sacred flow. Many people are ill-equipped to handle emotions or coach others as to how to handle them.

What we believe and think translates to our emotions. Our emotions and how we handle them refer us back to our belief matrix. Our story has taught us how to express or not express emotions. Emotions are responders, our soul's mouthpiece. Often we harshly criticize our emotions and the emotions of others. But emotions aren't necessarily good or bad. They are reflective, and therefore can serve as valuable assets.

One simple yet helpful illustration I've heard relates emotions as dashboard indicator lights, like *low fuel* or *check engine.* These lights aid and protect us, preventing real internal damage or breakdown. When these dash lights appear, it's ridiculous to be upset with the light itself. The real issue lies within the car somewhere. We would be wise to be thankful for the light, pull over, and deal with the deeper issue. This is not to suggest that emotions be managed mechanically. We need to embrace emotions, even the rawest of emotions, and move beneath them to what is empowering them.

Emotions have the potential to serve as one of our most powerful allies in our sacred flow with God. They offer feedback by disclosing our current focus. They take us back to our belief matrix, reflecting what is going on under our hood. Subsequently, we are able to deal with root issues. If we embrace our emotions and invite God to process them with us, we are able to maintain a healthy posture and continue flowing. If we ignore our emotions, eventually we break down, flowless, with untold internal damage.

One day a couple of years ago I came home from work early and noticed a police car in my neighbor's driveway. My neighbor's wife, Emma, was outside talking to the police and other neighbors. I thought maybe their house had been burglarized, so I walked over. To my dismay it was much worse, my neighbor's husband was missing. He had been since the evening before. The situation quickly

> **Faith does not operate in the realm of the possible. There is no glory for God in that which is humanly possible. Faith begins where man's power ends.**
>
> *George Muller*

became surreal. Ed was a good friend and a good man. He and I talked regularly. As a kindhearted neighbor and professional electrician, he was helping me with construction in my basement. A day or two earlier my wife and I had just been talking about Ed's care and compassion for others. Under a strange set of circumstances, Ed drowned in the lake behind his house. It took a week to find him. It was an awful week. The investigation proved Ed's death to be a freak accident. Ed left behind a wife, a college aged daughter and a teenage daughter and son.

Needless to say, this wrecked my flow. I was writing this book at the time. I stopped. I was numb. For weeks I couldn't even bring myself to go down in my basement where Ed and I had been working. Some of his tools were still there. My wife and I reeled for months. We felt angry, sad, confused, and disappointed. God felt distant and uncaring. We hurt for the loss of a friend and we hurt for his family. We couldn't imagine the intensity of the pain Emma and her kids must have been feeling. Questions flooded us. How could this happen? To him? Why? Why this way? Why now? What does this mean? In light of tragedy, does sacred flow even matter? Is it valid here? Now?

Grace grows best in winter.
Samuel Rutherford

I allowed myself to feel. I processed a lot. Time crawled ahead. I came to the realization that if sacred flow isn't valid in ugly painful places then it's not valid anywhere. I came to realize that our sacred flow includes mourning. I offered my sorrow to God, I asked him to bring me back to the truth, reposition my posture, and move me onward in his flow. Despite what our story has taught us, embracing and expressing emotion is essential. With great courage we stay aware, vulnerable, and focused on God in the midst of unrelenting pain. We process and flow into and through our pain and numbness. Sure, we will be knocked around and have to find our way back to flow, but we can still hold on to the roots of flow during our pain or suffering. It's beneficial to do so. The same pain that disrupts our sacred flow has the potential to deepen it.

It takes courage to live into the sacred flow. Primarily, we've got to come clean with God and ourselves. Our sacred flow deepens as we offer God all of the baggage in our lives. He will unpack it, sort the contents, and fold them into our future. This includes our false or irrational beliefs about any and everything and our go-to coping rhythms. These things do not define us, God's love does. God leads us to walk away from these things or let them go in order more fully experience who we are in his sacred flow.

***

In the 2000 Robert Redford film, *The Legend of Bagger Vance,* golf serves as metaphor for life and actor Will Smith, as Bagger Vance, characterizes God. Vagabond Bagger becomes a sage-like caddy for the main character Rannulph Junuh played by Matt Damon. Throughout the movie Bagger clubs Junuh with healing nuggets of divine truth. Junuh, once a golf protégé and champion, now years later, suffers from severe psychological wounds related to his service in World War I. He is given an opportunity to play golf again, but his game reflects his miserable soul. His flow is long gone.

During their first meeting Bagger tells Junuh that he has *lost his swing* and the two of them will have to go find it. His swing is out there somewhere in the harmony of all that was, is, and will be. Bagger expounds more about this to his young assistant Hardy,

> Yep, inside each and every one of us is one true, authentic swing. Something we was born with, that's ours...and ours alone. Something can't be taught to you or learned. Something that got to be remembered. Over time, the world can rob us of that swing...and get buried inside us under...all our woulda's and coulda's, and shoulda's. Some folk even forget what their swing was like...[211]

Junuh lost his way...his sacred flow...his swing. He was stuck in the past, without hope for the future. Life had robbed him of rhythm, his authentic swing.

Maybe you can relate to Junuh.

Bagger explains that we all have an authentic swing, *a flow,* that is our and ours alone. This swing is both innate and God-given. As we flow in the divine current we discover ourselves, our rhythm within God's rhythm, our authentic swing.

In a poignant scene Bagger speaks to Junuh about releasing his burden and remembering his flow.

> Bagger: Time to go on, lay it down.
> Junuh: I don't know how.
> Bagger: You got a choice. You can stop...or you could start.
> Junuh: Start?
> Bagger: Walking.
> Junuh: Where?
> Bagger: Back to where you've been and then stand there. Still.
>   Real still, and remember.
> Junuh: It was too long ago.
> Bagger: No, sir, it was just a moment ago. Time to come on out the shadows, Junuh.
> Time for you to choose.
> Junuh: I can't.
> Bagger: You can. You ain't alone. I'm right here with you. I've been here all along.

To get our swing back or find our flow we've got to lay down our burdens – release to God whatever has been weighing us down. Like Junuh, it's time for us to choose. We can continue pushing our rock or we can lean back and lie still, real still, in the sacred flow. God is with us, has been all along.

Benediction

It's time for your faith to flow. A flowing faith will
continually awaken you to the fact that your life resides in God's
infusive love. You have been blessed and sent out by God's love
in the Spirit-walking way of Jesus. As Jesus approached death on
the cross he prayed for his friends. He asked the Father to set
them apart in the truth and then he sent them out as he was sent
out. "As you sent Me into the world, I also have sent them into
the world."[212] Being sent out in the way of Jesus means being
sent out to live the way that Jesus modeled – a life that flows
from God the Father. Jesus calls us to a life of total abandonment
to the will of the Father through power of the Spirit. You've been
ushered into Jesus' relationship with the Father. Follow his inner
voice of love. This voice will lead you to go about as Jesus did,
loving God and others as you love yourself.

Empowered by the Spirit, continue the work the Father
gave Jesus to do. Tell the good news of God's grace to the poor
(everyone). Share God's freedom with those who are trapped or
imprisoned. Proclaim clarity and sight to those who are
confused and blind. Fight for those who are downtrodden or
trampled. Let everyone know God's favor is present in the here
and now.[213] Let the love of God flow through you like a torrent.

Allow nothing to prevent you from diving into God's
sacred flow. Don't let dogma, institution, legalism, pain from
your past or present, fear of the future, or your fallen flesh
distract you from finding your focus, choosing your challenge,
or following your feedback. You are dead to sin, the flesh, the
Law, but alive to God! Christ lives in you. In any way and every
way possible open yourself to the *Logos*-life that pressures you
from within and without. Live pragmystically. Be formed by
God's flow. Absorb God; be saturated in him so that you know
restful rhythm despite what life brings you. Fearlessly risk,
trusting God to provide you with more than enough inspiration,
courage, and capability to do so. Dive into life and lay back in
the divine current.

Finally, in the words of Bagger Vance,

Now play the game.
Your game...the one that God meant only you to play.
The one given to you when you were born.
Come on, take your stance...don't hold anything back.

You're ready...now's the time.

It's time for your faith to flow.

Appendix

Practicing Grace

I've started and stopped a routine of spiritual practices hundreds of times. My consistency lasts a week, a month, or at most a few months. I taper off, feel guilty, taper more, feel more guilty...and finally drop the practice or practices altogether. As I've learned to live in the divine current I've changed my approach to the spiritual practices. Now I recognize the spiritual practices as rhythms of grace. They are meant to happen rhythmically without guilt or shame. They are gifts that help us become more attuned with God, ourselves, and others. They mean to keep us in step with the Spirit by helping us be fully available, focused, and engaged with God moment by moment. The practices help us pose and re-pose. They teach us how to better swim along in God's current.

Offering another image, a flow-ready soul posture hoists our sails and sets them in order to harness the Spirit. Spiritual practices aid in holding the sails in place and trim the sails, fine tuning our collection of the most powerful energy available to us. Our posture and the practices ebb and flow with each other. A flow-ready posture leads to and strengthens the practices while the practices tweak our soul pose promoting better flow. Both readily lead us back to the roots that foster our sacred flow. All of the spiritual practices double as ways of being. We may approach them as distinct rhythms and as a way of life within sacred flow.

Regarding the explanation of spiritual practices below, my intention is not be comprehensive in scope or depth. I simply want to (re)introduce these practices in connection with sacred flow.

prayer

Prayer anchors our daily life and all of the spiritual practices in God's presence. Commonly, we refer to prayer as conversation with God. Henri Nouwen called this conversation "the hub of life, the center of all life and all love."[214] Sacred flow's focus, challenge, and feedback require far more just talking *at* God. Prayer happens in many different forms. The most notable and useful practices in the context of sacred flow are described below. They range from distinct structured practices to an unceasing or flowing lifestyle of prayer. In essence, prayer begets sacred flow and sacred flow begets prayer.

simple prayer

I borrowed this terminology, *simple prayer*, from Richard Foster. [215] This is the form of prayer with which most of us are accustomed. We conversationally speak to God internally or aloud making requests or offering thanksgiving, praise, etc. Simple prayer can also be a time of confession and repentance during which we agree with God about our fleshly flow and intentionally re-turn our soul to God. In simple prayer, we plainly pour out our heart and soul to God. We have come to our senses, returned to the land of the living and the sacred flow.

silence/solitude

Silence de-fragments our soul. It allows us to stop in the midst of life's hustle and bustle and regain internal unity, *re-collect*. Several forms of practicing silence can be helpful. We may be prayerfully silent by simply not talking while among people. We may choose to shut off the car radio during our commute or turn off the television at home. Or we may intentionally choose to pull away to a silent place. In silence, our minds can be empty or occupied with supplication, thanksgiving, adoration, etc. Silence leads to slowing and inner stillness – a sorely needed calming of our spirit, soul, and body.

Silence is a potent practice that teaches us to speak and live powerfully.[216] It opens us to hear what God would have us do or say. Silence helps us to work through our thoughts and emotions so that we respond meaningfully and rhythmically rather than react irresponsibly.

Solitude is a partner of silence. Solitude takes us further into silence as we extract ourselves from others. Solitude has been called the furnace of transformation. Without ample time in solitude we suffer as victims of our culture, our false self, and fleshly flow.[217] All alone in lonely places we are stripped of our self-protective weapons, and left to wrestle God and our false self. Like Jacob we usually come away with a holy limp. In solitude we may choose to not think at all or intensively think through those things that have been disturbing our soul. Either way, it benefits us to regularly pull away to a lonesome place for spirit, soul, or body restoration.

Moreover, Richard Foster contends that solitude is not only the occasional event of withdrawing to lonely places; it is an ongoing disposition of inner stillness.[218] Even in the midst of others, we may remain inwardly still or withdrawn, allowing God to continue his work. Solitude serves as a useful practice to reawaken awareness and regain our rhythm within God's.

sacred word

The sacred word, prayer word, or breath prayer is a word or a short sentence that helps us center our attention in order to regain focus. Thomas Keating asserted, "The sacred word enables you to sink into your Source."[219] It can be words or short phrases like any of the following; *God, Jesus, Spirit, peace, grace, love, cease striving, be still, My Jesus, Thank you Jesus,* etc. The word is spoken internally or quietly aloud in rhythm with our breathing. Some version of the ancient Jesus Prayer, also called the Prayer of the Heart, born out of the Eastern Orthodox Church may also be used, "Lord Jesus Christ, Son of God, have mercy on me."[220] Any time distraction occurs during silent meditation or in everyday life, the sacred word leads our attention back to God. The sacred word serves as our centering resource in the midst of the mundane or madness in our workplace or at home…or anywhere else.

meditation/contemplation

Meditation is prayerful pondering, listening prayer. When we meditate, we intentionally invite God to saturate our thoughts. Beyond raw introspection, we trust God to enter and settle our muddy mind. During meditation, we may mull over scriptures, other reading, images, life's circumstances, nature, etc. with sensitivity to the presence of God and more specifically, his voice. Meditation is a balancing act between attention and relaxation.[221] Meditation moves us from a superficial consciousness to a meditative or interior consciousness.[222] With this open-focus our perspective begins to change. Our soul's movement toward experiencing union and rhythm with God provides the primary intent and content of our meditation. Living a meditative life means living slowly, intentionally, mindfully, and reflectively.

Meditative prayer may lead deeper to contemplation, centering prayer. Contemplation is a wide-souled waiting for a wordless resonance with God.[223] It has been described as two lovers electrified in the presence of one another without the need to say a word.[224] The contemplative norm is not ecstatic experience, but a profound simple attention. Contemplation postures us to truly experience God. It opens us to experience the inflow of God's love.[225] Contemplation may range from centering prayer to a lifestyle reflective of sacred flow. Sacred flow leads us to daily and deeply resonate with God despite our circumstances.

daily examen

The daily examen is a meditative prayer in which we reflect upon the content our day. It has us take stock at the end of each day or week. We take time to reflect, considering when and how we've experienced God or haven't. This might also be a time in which we ask God to examine our soul. The examen nurtures our attentiveness to the presence and movement of God in our daily life.

lectio divina

Sometimes called sacred reading, prayer reading, or meditative reading, *lectio divina* is the reading of the Scriptures very slowly with sensitive awareness. While reading, we stop anytime God seems to be highlighting a word or phrase. We then meditate or chew upon this word or phrase until God releases us to continue reading. We may use this practice for months on a single verse, wringing from it anything and everything God would like to reveal. Taking the practice beyond

Scriptures, lectio divina may be creatively practiced using images, nature, film, music, circumstances, etc. Lectio divina asks us to slow down our perception allowing God to infuse it, open it, mold it and surprise us with new revelation. Lectio divina opens our understanding and experience of God's mysterious flow that lies beneath the surface of the Scriptures, images, nature, film, music, etc.

unceasing prayer

Unceasing prayer is the extemporaneous prayer called for by Paul in 1 Thessalonians 5: 17, "pray without ceasing." As we go about our daily life, we talk with and listen to God about anything and everything. We bear others' burdens and bless them as we go about our business. Unceasing prayer is a normative practice in sacred flow. With an open-focus we carry on an endless sacred conversation…with or without audible words. We widen our perception to collect anything God would have us pray while we continually focus on him, his love, and his love being manifested through us. Our life becomes a spontaneous flowing prayer.

study

Study is another significant spiritual practice. Learning often leads us deeper into reality and therefore deeper into God's sacred flow. Fittingly, Richard Foster relates biblical study as "an analytical search for the perception of reality in a given context."[226] This realistic perception provides wisdom for our journey. Studying the scriptures, commentaries, books, etc. creates diverse opportunities for God to bring us more revelation, wisdom, and awareness. Broad study introduces us to a wide portfolio of information through which God speaks. Certainly, spiritual study is anchored in the Scriptures but it benefits us greatly to venture into art, culture, history, media, design, and other fields. As noted in an earlier chapter, sacred flow inspires spiritual learning and unlearning. As we flow with God, we study as a spiritual practice and way of life.

worship

John records Jesus saying the time has come for God's people to worship in spirit and in truth. The word worship in Greek, *proskuneo*, means *to bend, fawn* or *crouch* and *to kiss*…as a dog kisses or laps his master's hand. We kneel to kiss, adore, and reverence God in *spirit*, from deep within.[227] As our inward disposition (spirit) continually kisses God, it profoundly affects our outward disposition. Also, we aim to worship in *truth*. We open ourselves to kiss the God of reality, not one we may have falsely manufactured and idolize. Authentic worship means laying aside our preconceived notions and worshiping freely, kissing the ever-present, ever-revealing God. Inwardly and outwardly, bending and standing upright, we gratefully acknowledge God's presence, goodness, and sovereignty.

Given this description, worship may encompass widely varying content and contexts. Unfortunately, worship often gets relegated to an hour or so on Sunday. Even worse, worship becomes limited to the few songs that typically open the Sunday gathering. Too often worship feels contrived and forced. Thankfully, worship doesn't have to be squelched and squished into a performance. Worship happens anytime anywhere. Sacred flow leads us into unceasing worship. While flowing, we continually revere God with our focused attention upon him in the moment at hand. We sacredly *re-pose* to kiss God continually with our whole life. Worship, as a practice or a lifestyle, inspires awareness and facilitates the mind being set on God and divine love.

simplicity

The practice of simplicity betrays the distraction, compulsion, and materialism embedded in our environment. Practically anything can distract us. We easily accumulate potentially distracting possessions and habits. Simplicity allows us to freely and fully engage God without over-concern for a million superficial possessions, habits, or affairs of little consequence. Simplicity leads us to purge those things we don't really need. It removes the burdensome pile smothering our soul. Thus, the practice of simplicity, like surrender, is a practice of peeling. With the Spirit's guidance and power, we peel away those things that hinder or prevent our sacred flow. Simplicity resets our priorities, releasing our mind to be set on more significant matters like love.

journaling

Writing affords us the opportunity to download our soul. Expressing ourselves through writing creates disc space for God to *refill*. It helps us unpack or untangle our emotions, coping rhythms, and underlying beliefs as well as invite God to speak into them. Journaling provides space for us to process our flow experiences – sacred or fleshly. It can be used for prayer, in silence, meditation, lectio divina, daily examen, etc. It can be used for study, fasting, or simply as a daily diary. Journaling transforms our soul posture into a tangible, reflective outlet that keeps us attuned to God's Spirit.

Journaling easily integrates into our daily lifestyle if we carry a small pocket notebook or use the notepad on our phone. When thoughts, emotions, words, or impressions worthy of journaling surface within us, we stop and jot them down. Lifestyle journaling extends the journaling practice into each moment providing another way for us the respond to the Spirit's feedback.

fasting

Fasting teaches us about dependence, gratitude, and provision. God may lead us to fast in order to teach us about our capacity to go on without *it*, whatever *it* happens to be. Fasting, like simplicity, resets our priorities. God calls us to fast as a way to reinstate himself as our Source. By no means is fasting limited to food. We may be led to fast television, recreation, chocolate, our blackberry or iphone, sex, beer, gaming, internet usage, etc. As odd as it may seem, fasting may become a lifestyle. We may rhythmically fast certain things as a way of life. In any case, fasting awakens and establishes priorities. Fasting resets our intimacy with God as our top priority. This level of surrender and focus fosters sacred flow.

community

Many of us have bounced in and out of spiritual community, myself included. We may be out of touch with it, but we long for community when we don't have it. Community is a spiritual practice because truly engaging with people requires *practice*. Community necessitates devoted intention. Living in a spiritual community can be messy and annoying. But just as the rhythm of the Spirit leads us to practice solitude, it leads us to community. Healthy Christian spirituality includes a faith community that helps us live out our daily life in the sacred flow.[228] In community, our individual rhythms become instruments of divine influence. Community provides an opportunity for God to amplify his love through each of us.

celebration

Holy parties are spiritual practices. Celebration is sacred. For example, God commanded the Feast of the Tabernacles as a mandated seven-day party celebrating Israel's exodus from Egypt. It's still celebrated today.

> *On the fifteenth day of the seventh month, hold a*
> *sacred assembly and do no regular work. Celebrate*
> *a festival to the LORD for seven days.*
> *Numbers 29: 12*

Celebration is serious business according to God. Celebration can be considered a practice of gratitude and worship. It provides an outlet for us to express our joy related to being united with God and each other. This practice needs prayerful priority since it so easily gets trivialized, perverted, or neglected. Most of us need to party better and more often. Celebration may also merge into our way of life as joy envelops our life. This would de-categorize celebration releasing our whole life to be an artful celebration of our union with God and our freedom to flow.

sabbath

God knows we need rest, especially since we live in such a harried culture. As we flow with the Father we will creatively observe rest. Our rhythmic engagement leads us to regularly engage in release, recovery, and rest. Performance psychologists Jim Loehr and Tony Schwartz, support the Sabbath ideal in saying, "Performance, health, and happiness are grounded in the skillful management of energy."[229] Rhythmically spending and restoring energy is the key to healthy and optimal performance. God leads us to pull aside to rest and recover spirit, soul, and body. Slowing down, we re-collect God's loving presence and the energy needed to continue flowing. As we live attuned God, we sense when it's time to slow down, rest, and recover....not only on Sunday afternoons.

As addressed in chapter eleven, Sabbath becomes our way of life within God's flow. This deserves revisiting. We live in a Sabbath covenant or paradigm. Every day is set aside for worship. Living in a Sabbath paradigm means we trust in the sufficiency and divine energy of Christ to accomplish all things in and through us. We work to enter and remain in a promised rest. The writer of Hebrews encourages, "let us be diligent to enter that rest [God's rest], so that no one will fall, through following the same example of disobedience [Israel]"[230] Doing anything in and of our own strength, to meet our needs apart from God is *anti-sabbath,* disobedient, fleshly flow. Our movement is meant to be restful and life-giving, sourced by the Spirit of flow. We're meant to maintain as Sabbath lifestyle.

service

I hesitate to include service as a spiritual 'practice.' In minimizing service to a practice I risk minimizing the mission of God. Service and God's love are inseparable. The gospel *is* service. Our spiritual DNA naturally manifests service. In essence, to serve someone is to submit to them. To live into the sacred flow we submit or entrust ourselves to God in each moment. This submission extends to our neighbors, as we love them as God loves them. Engaging service as a spiritual practice can open our hearts and minds to other people and service as a way of life. What we can actually do in the course of a few hours or a day of service is limited, but what it can do to us is immeasurable.

All of the spiritual practices above serve as avenues of engagement, tools to be used rhythmically to nurture sacred flow. They supplement one another and give tangible expression to a flow-ready posture and the roots of sacred flow. They are valuable rhythms for a flowing faith.

Bibliography

Augsburger, David. *Dissident Discipleship: A Spirituality of Self-Surrender, Love of God, and Love of Neighbor.* Grand Rapids, MI: Brazos Press, 2006.

Belitz, Charlene, and Meg Lundstrom. *The Power of Flow; Practical Ways to Transform Your Life with Meaningful Coincidence.* New York: Three Rivers Press, 1998.

Benner, David G. *Sacred Companions: The Gift of Spiritual Friendship & Direction.* Downers Grove, IL: InterVarsity Press, 2002.

Bloesch, Donald. *Spirituality Old & New; Recovering Authentic Spiritual Life.* Downers Grove, IL: IVP Academic, 2007.

Bonhoeffer, Dietrich. *The Cost of Discipleship.* New York, NY: Macmillan Publishing Co., 1963.

Campbell, James M. *Paul the Mystic.* New York: Andrew Melrose, 1907.

Campolo, Anthony. *The God of Intimacy and Action; Reconnecting Ancient Spiritual Practices, Evangelism, and Justice.* San Francisco, CA: Jossey-Bass, 2007.

Chamberlin, Jamie. "Reaching Flow to Optimize Work and Play." *American Psychological Association Monitor* 29, no. 7 (1998).

Clement, Olivier. *The Roots of Christian Mysticism.* London, UK: New City, 1995.

Cooper, Andrew. *Playing in the Zone: Exploring the Spiritual Dimensions of Sports.* Boston, MA: Shambhala Publication, Inc, 1998.

Cox, Harvey G. Jr. "Make Way for the Spirit." In *God's Life in Trinity*, ed. Miroslav Volf and Michael Welker, 93-100. Minneapolis, MN: Fortress Press, 2006.

Csikszentmihalyi, Mihaly. *Flow: The Psychology of Optimal Experience*. New York, NY: Harper & Row, 1990.

_____. *Creativity: Flow and the Psychology of Discovery and Invention*. New York: HarperPerennial, 1996.

_____. *Finding Flow: The Psychology of Engagement with Everyday Life*. New York, NY: BasicBooks, 1997.

De Caussade, Jean-Pierre. *Abandonment to Divine Providence*. New York: Image Books, 1975.

Dumm, Demetrius. *A Mystical Portrait of Jesus: New Perspectives on John's Gospel*. Collegeville, MN: The Liturgical Press, 2001.

Dunn, James D. G. ed. *Paul and the Mosaic Law*. Grand Rapids, MI: Williams B. Eerdmans Publishing Company, 1996.

_____. *Jesus and the Spirit: A Study of the Religious and Charismatic Experience of Jesus and the First Christians as Reflected in the New Testament*. Grand Rapids, MI: Wm B. Eerdmans Publishing Co., 1997.

Dupré, Louis. *The Deeper Life: An Introduction to Christian Mysticism*. New York, NY: Crossroad, 1981.

Dupré, Louis, and O.S.B. James A. Wiseman. *Light from Light: An Anthology of Christian Mysticism*. 2nd ed. New York, NY: Paulist Press, 2001.

Eastman, Brad. *The Significance of Grace in the Letters of Paul*. New York, NY: Peter Lang, 1999.

Egan, Harvey S.J. *An Anthology of Christian Mysticism*. Collegeville, MN: The Liturgical Press, 1991.

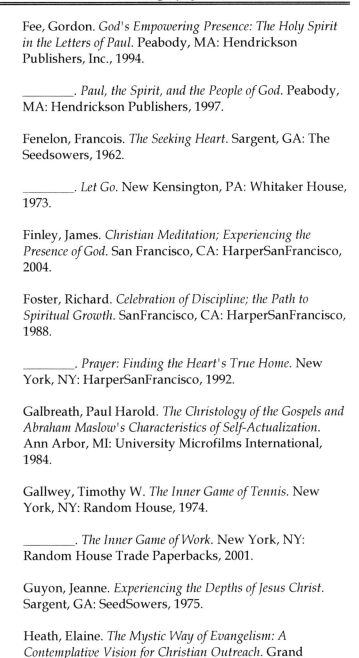

Fee, Gordon. *God's Empowering Presence: The Holy Spirit in the Letters of Paul.* Peabody, MA: Hendrickson Publishers, Inc., 1994.

_____. *Paul, the Spirit, and the People of God.* Peabody, MA: Hendrickson Publishers, 1997.

Fenelon, Francois. *The Seeking Heart.* Sargent, GA: The Seedsowers, 1962.

_____. *Let Go.* New Kensington, PA: Whitaker House, 1973.

Finley, James. *Christian Meditation; Experiencing the Presence of God.* San Francisco, CA: HarperSanFrancisco, 2004.

Foster, Richard. *Celebration of Discipline; the Path to Spiritual Growth.* SanFrancisco, CA: HarperSanFrancisco, 1988.

_____. *Prayer: Finding the Heart's True Home.* New York, NY: HarperSanFrancisco, 1992.

Galbreath, Paul Harold. *The Christology of the Gospels and Abraham Maslow's Characteristics of Self-Actualization.* Ann Arbor, MI: University Microfilms International, 1984.

Gallwey, Timothy W. *The Inner Game of Tennis.* New York, NY: Random House, 1974.

_____. *The Inner Game of Work.* New York, NY: Random House Trade Paperbacks, 2001.

Guyon, Jeanne. *Experiencing the Depths of Jesus Christ.* Sargent, GA: SeedSowers, 1975.

Heath, Elaine. *The Mystic Way of Evangelism: A Contemplative Vision for Christian Outreach.* Grand Rapids, MI: Baker Academic, 2008.

Horsfall, Tony. *Rhythms of Grace: Finding Intimacy with God in a Busy Life*. Eastbourne, UK: Kingsway Publications, 2004.

Jackson, Susan, A. and Mihaly Csikszentmihalyi. *Flow in Sports: The Keys to Optimal Experiences and Performances*. Champaign, IL: Human Kinetics, 1999.

Johnston, William. *Mystical Theology: The Science of Love*. Maryknoll, NY: Orbis Books, 1995.

Jones, Tony. *The Sacred Way; Spiritual Practices for Everyday Life*. Grand Rapids, MI: Zondervan, 2005.

Keating, Thomas *Open Mind Open Heart: The Contemplative Dimension of the Gospel*. New York, NY: Continuum, 1997.

Kelly, Thomas. *A Testament of Devotion*. New York, NY: HarperOne, 1992.

Laubach, Frank. *Letters by a Modern Mystic*. Colorado Springs, CO: Purposeful Design Publications, 2007.

Lawrence, Brother. *The Practice of the Presence of God*. New Kensington, PA: Whitaker House, 1982.

Loehr, Jim, and Tony Schwartz. *The Power of Full Engagement: Managing Energy, Not Time, Is the Key to High Performance and Personal Renewal*. New York, NY: Free Press Paperbacks, 2003.

Macquarrie, John. *Two Worlds Are Ours: An Introduction to Christian Mysticism*. Minneapolis, MN: Fortress Press, 2005.

Maloney, George. *The Mystery of Christ in You: The Mystical Vision of Saint Paul*. New York: Alba House, 1998.

_____. *Abiding in the Indwelling Trinity*. New York: Paulist Press, 2004.

Maslow, Abraham H. "A Theory of Human Motivation." *Psychological Review* 50, no. L (1943): 370-396.

_____. *Toward a Psychology of Being*. New York, NY: Van Nostrand Reinhold Company, 1968.

_____. *The Further Reaches of Human Nature*. New York, NY: Penguin Group, 1976.

_____. *Religions, Values, and Peak-Experiences*. New York, NY: Penguin Compass, 1994.

May, Gerald, M.D. *Will and Spirit: A Contemplative Psychology*. New York, NY: HarperSanFrancisco, 1982.

_____. *Addiction & Grace: Love and Spirituality in the Healing of Addictions*. New York, NY: HarperSanFrancisco, 1988.

McIntosh, Mark. *Mystical Theology: The Integrity of Spirituality and Theology*. Malden, MA: Blackwell Publishers, 1998.

Merton, Thomas. *The New Man*. New York, NY: Farrar, Straus, & Cudahy, 1961.

_____. *New Seeds of Contemplation*. New York: New Directions Books, 1972.

_____. *The Ascent to Truth*. New York: Harcourt, Inc, 1981.

_____. *Thoughts in Solitude*. Boston, MA: Shambhala, 1993.

_____. *The Inner Experience*, ed. William H. Shannon. New York, NY: HarperSanFrancisco, 2003.

Murphy, Michael. *In the Zone: Transcendent Experience in Sports.* Harmondsworth, England: Penguin Books Ltd, 1995.

Murray, Andrew. *Absolute Surrender.* New Kensington, PA: Whitaker House, 1981.

_____. *Humility.* New Kensington, PA: Whitaker House, 1982.

_____. *Experiencing the Holy Spirit.* New Kensington, PA: Whitaker House, 1985.

_____. *Abiding in Christ.* Fort Washington, PA: Christian Literature Crusade, 1997.

Nee, Watchman. *The Release of the Spirit.* Indianapolis, IN: Sure Foundation Publishers, 1965.

_____. *The Spiritual Man.* New York, NY: Christian Fellowship Publishers, Inc., 1977.

_____. *Grace for Grace.* New York, NY: Christian Fellowship Publishers, Inc., 1983.

Nouwen, Henri J. M. *Making All Things New: An Invitation to the Spiritual Life.* New York, NY: HarperSanFrancisco, 1981.

_____. *Here and Now; Living in the Spirit.* New York, NY: Crossroad Publishing Company, 1994.

_____. *The Only Necessary Thing: Living a Prayerful Life.* New York, NY: Crossroad, 1999.

_____. *Life of the Beloved.* New York, NY: Crossroad, 2000.

_____. *Spiritual Direction: Wisdom for the Long Walk of Faith.* ed. Michael J. Christensen and Rebecca J. Laird. New York, NY: HarperSanFrancisco, 2006.

Pseudo-Dionysius. *Pseudo-Dionysius: The Complete Works.* Translated by Colm Luibheid. New York, NY: Paulist Press, 1987.

Ravizza, Ken. "Qualities of the Peak Experience in Sport." In *Psychological Foundations of Sport,* ed. J.M Silva and R.S. Weinberg, 452-462. Champaign, IL: Human Kinetics, 1984.

Scazzero, Peter. *Emotionally Healthy Spirituality.* Nashville, TN: Integrity Publishers, 2006.

Schweitzer, Albert. *The Mysticism of Paul the Apostle.* New York, NY: Henry Holt & Co., 1931.

Smith, Malcolm. *The Power of the Blood Covenant: Uncover the Secret Strength in God's Eternal Oath.* Tulsa, OK: Harrison House, 2002.

Stone, Dan, and Greg Smith. *The Rest of the Gospel: When the Partial Gospel Has Worn You Out.* Dallas, TX: One Press, 2000.

Sweet, Leonard. *Quantum Spirituality: A Postmodern Apologetic.* Dayton, OH: Whaleprints, 1994.

_____. *Postmodern Pilgrims; First Century Passion for the 21st Century World* Nashville, TN: Broadman & Holdman Publishers, 2000.

Thomas, Major Ian. *The Saving Life of Christ and The Mystery of Godliness.* Grand Rapids, MI: Zondervan, 1988.

Torrance, Thomas F. *The Christian Doctrine of God; One Being Three Persons.* Edinburgh, UK: T & T Clark, 1996.

Underhill, Evelyn. *Mysticism: A Study in the Nature and Development of Man's Spiritual Consciousness.* New York, NY: E. P. Dutton, 1912.

_____. *Practical Mysticism: A Little Book for Normal People*. Columbus, OH: Ariel Press, 1986.

Volf, Miroslav and Michael Welker, eds. *God's Life in the Trinity*. Minneapolis, MN: Fortress Press, 2006.

Wiseman, James A. *Spirituality and Mysticism*. Maryknoll, NY: Orbis Books, 2006.

Wright, N. T. *Simply Christian: Why Christianity Makes Sense*. New York, NY: Harper One, 2006.

Notes

Introduction: Finding Flow

[1] U2, "I Still Haven't Found What I'm Looking For," *The Joshua Tree*, Island Records, 1987.

[2] Susan Jackson and Mihaly Csikszentmihalyi, *Flow in Sports: The Keys to Optimal Experiences and Performances* (Champaign, IL: Human Kinetics, 1999), 12.

Chapter 1: Religious Woes or a Faith That Flows?

[3] Galatians 2: 20.

[4] Rhythm, http://dictionary.reference.com/browse/rhythm, (accessed August 10, 2008).

[5] Ibid.

[6] Abraham Maslow, *Religions, Values, and Peak-Experiences* (New York, NY: Penguin Compass, 1994), xv.

[7] Religion, http://dictionary.reference.com/browse/religion (accessed October 03, 2008).

[8] Psalm 111: 10, Proverbs 1: 7, 9: 10, 15: 33.

[9] Abraham Maslow, *Religions, Values, and Peak-Experiences*, 24.

[10] Mihaly Csikszentmihalyi, *Flow: The Psychology of Optimal Experience* (New York, NY: Harper & Row, 1990), 238.

[11] Ibid.

[12] Online Parallel Bible Project, "Greek Lexicon; rest." www.biblos.com, http://strongsnumbers.com/greek/373.htm (accessed May 25, 2008).

[13] Ibid.

[14] John 7: 38.

Chapter 2: Dive into the Flow

[15] Csikszentmihalyi did sampling studies and scores of interviews that included cross-cultural subjects. Mihaly Csikszentmihalyi, *The Evolving Self: A Psychology for the Third Millennium* (New York: HarperPerennial, 1993), 358.

[16] Csikszentmihalyi, *Flow*, 4.

[17] Jackson and Csikszentmihalyi, *Flow in Sports*, 5.

[18] Csikszentmihalyi, *Flow*, 4.

[19] Ibid, 2-8.

[20] Abraham H. Maslow, *Religions, Values, and Peak-Experiences*, 5.

[21] Abraham H. Maslow, *Toward a Psychology of Being* (New York, NY: Van Nostrand Reinhold Company, 1968), 16.

[22] Csikszentmihalyi, *Flow*, 71-77.

[23] Timothy Gallwey, *The Inner Game of Work* (New York, NY: Random House Trade Paperbacks, 2001), 57.

[24] Mihaly Csikszentmihalyi, *Finding Flow: The Psychology of Engagement with Everyday Life* (New York, NY: BasicBooks, 1997), 117.

[25] Mihaly Csikszentmihalyi, *Creativity: Flow and the Psychology of Discovery and Invention* (New York: HarperPerennial, 1996), 114.

[26] Mihaly Csikszentmihalyi, Sami Abuhamdeh, and Jeanne Nakamura *Flow*, http://academic.udayton.edu/jackbauer/ CsikFlow.pdf (accessed June 4, 2008).

[27] Jackson and Csikszentmihalyi, *Flow in Sports*, 6.

[28] Csikszentmihalyi, *Flow*, 216.

[29] Ibid, 228.

[30] Jackson and Csikszentmihalyi, *Flow in Sports*, 22.

[31] Ibid, 118.

[32] Csikszentmihalyi, *Flow*, 99.

[33] Michael Murphy, *In the Zone: Transcendent Experience in Sports* (Harmondsworth, England: Penguin Books Ltd, 1995), 9-66. Csikszentmihalyi, *Flow*, 48-70. Maslow, *Religions, Values, and Peak-Experiences*, 59-68.

34 Andrew Cooper, *Playing in the Zone: Exploring the Spiritual Dimensions of Sports* (Boston: Shambhala Publication, 1998), 33.

35 Maslow, *Religions, Values, and Peak-Experiences*, 59.

36 Abraham H. Maslow, *Toward a Psychology of Being* (New York, NY: Van Nostrand Reinhold Company, 1968), 79.

37 Ibid, 80.

38 Maslow, *Religions, Values, and Peak-Experiences*, 67.

39 Maslow, *Toward a Psychology of Being*, 111.

40 Abraham H. Maslow, *The Further Reaches of Human Nature* (New York, NY: Penguin Group, 1976), 60.

41 Mihaly Csikszentmihalyi, *Finding Flow: The Psychology of Engagement with Everyday Life* (New York, NY: BasicBooks, 1997), 34.

42 D. Mezmer, *The Flow Experience: The Summa Cum Lousy of Bad Psychology*. http://flowstate.homestead. com/files/zflowlousy.htm (accessed March 20, 2008).

43 http://en.wikipedia.org/wiki/Dopamine (accessed October 23, 2010).

44 Murphy, *In the Zone*, 11.

45 Csikszentmihalyi, *Flow*, 49.

46 Murphy, *In the Zone*. 24.

47 Maslow, *Religions, Values, and Peak-Experiences*, 67.

48 Tim Gallway, The *Inner Game of Work*, 44.

49 Csikszentmihalyi, *Flow*, 64.

50 Ibid, 49.

Chapter 3: Jesus Flows

51 George Maloney, *Discovering the Hidden Reality: A Journey into Christian Mystical Prayer* (Staten Island, NY: Society of St. Paul, 2004), 116.

52 Leonard Sweet, *Quantum Spirituality: A Postmodern Apologetic* (Dayton, OH: Whaleprints, 1994), 62.

53 F.F. Bruce, *The Gospel of John: Introduction, Exposition, and Notes* (Grand Rapids, MI: William B. Eerdmans Publishing Company, 1983), 29.

54 Ibid.

[55] Barclay Newman, and Eugene Nida, *A Handbook on The Gospel of John* (New York, NY: United Bible Societies, 1980), 7.

[56] Sweet, *Quantum Spirituality*, 62.

[57] Colossians 1: 15-17, Revelation 21: 6.

[58] Sweet, *Quantum Spirituality*, 68.

[59] John 1: 4.

[60] Evelyn Underhill, *The Mystic Way: A Psychological Study in Christian Origins* (New York, NY: J.M. Dent & Sons, LTD., 1913), 222.

[61] Miroslav Volf and Michael Welker, eds. *God's Life in the Trinity* (Fortress Press: Minneapolis, MN, 2006), 11.

[62] Wilson Paroschi, *Incarnation and Covenant in the Prologue to the Fourth Gospel (John 1:18)*. 2006, (New York, NY: Peter Lang, 2006), 39.

[63] Colossians 2: 9, Colossians 1: 15-17, 19.

[64] This accommodates the concept of perichoresis (mutual interpenetration) – individuality and co-penetration of life and appropriation. Each person of the Trinity is involved in every outward action of the Godhead. Alister McGrath, *Christian Theology*, Second Edition ed. 1997, (Cambridge, MA: Blackwell Publishers, 1997), 299.

[65] Thomas F. Torrance, *The Christian Doctrine of God; One Being Three Persons* (Edinburgh, UK: T & T Clark, 1996), 17.

[66] John 14: 20.

[67] John 14: 11, 20, 6: 57, 12: 45, 8: 29, 17: 22.

[68] A.T. Lincoln, *The Gospel According to Saint John* (Black's New Testament Commentaries, ed. M.D. Hooker. New York, NY: Continuum, 2005), 202.

[69] Ibid, 229.

[70] Ibid.

[71] G.E. Ladd, *A Theology of the New Testament* (Grand Rapids, MI: William B. Eerdmans Publishing Company, 1996), 285.

[72] Luke 19: 1-6.

[73] John 13: 3-10

[74] Hebrews 12: 2.

[75] 1 John 1: 2.

Chapter 4: The Flow Within

[76] Timothy Joyce, *Celtic Christianity: A Sacred Tradition, a Vision of Hope* (Maryknoll, NY: Orbis Books, 2007), 25, 154.

[77] A.W. Tozer, *The Pursuit of God* (Camp Hill, PA: Christian Publications, 1993), 77.

[78] John 14:20, New Living Translation.

[79] 2 Corinthians 2:15.

[80] Parallel Bible, "Greek Lexicon" http://strongsnumbers.com/greek/3466.htm (accessed May 23, 2008). Rick Meyers, *e-Sword* (Equipping Ministries Foundation: Franklin, TN, 2005), mystery.

[81] Colossians 3: 4.

[82] Philippians 1: 21, Philippians 2:13, Colossians 3: 3 - 4, Galatians 2: 20, Colossians 1: 29.

[83] John 8: 32.

[84] Incarnation, http://dictionary.reference.com/browse/ incarnation, (May 15, 2008).

[85] Galatians 2: 20, John 14: 20.

[86] 1 John 14: 15.

[87] 1 Corinthians 1: 30.

[88] Henry Cloud and John Townsend, *How People Grow; What the Bible Reveals About Personal Growth* (Grand Rapids, MI: Zondervan, 2001) 36.

[89] 1 Corinthians 6: 17.

[90] Romans 6:6, Galatians 2: 20.

[91] Parallel Bible, *Greek Lexicon, crucified with,* http://strongsnumbers.com/greek/4957.htm. Galatians 2: 20.

[92] F.F. Bruce, *Romans* (Tyndale New Testament Commentaries, ed. C.L. Morris. Grand Rapids, MI: William B. Eerdmans Publishing Company, 1987), 131.

[93] Parallel Bible, *Greek Lexicon; baptizo,* http://strongsnumbers.com/greek/907.htm. Romans 6: 3.

[94] Meyers, *e-Sword*, Romans 6:3.

[95] Connate, http://dictionary.reference.com/browse /connate (accessed May 23, 2008).

[96] Parallel Bible, *Greek Lexicon; in,* http://strongsnumbers.com/greek/1722.htm.

[97] 1 Corinthians 6: 19.

[98] Parenthesis contents mine.

[99] Parallel Bible, *Hebrew Lexicon; heart*, http://strongsnumbers.com/hebrew/3820.htm.

[100] Jeremiah 17: 9.

Chapter 5: Our Freedom to Flow

[101] 2 Corinthians 12:9.

[102] Scott Brittin, "Law vs. Grace," (lecture, Grace Ministries International, Atlanta, GA, November 12, 1999).

[103] Romans 6: 11, 7: 4.

[104] Malcolm Smith, *The Power of the Blood Covenant: Uncover the Secret Strength in God's Eternal Oath* (Tulsa, OK: Harrison House, 2002), 12.

[105] Hebrews 7-10.

[106] Hebrews 7: 23, 24, 26, 28.

[107] Hebrews 9: 24-26, 10: 10.

[108] Hebrews 7: 12.

[109] John 1: 17.

[110] Matthew 5: 17.

[111] Hebrews 8: 13.

[112] Hebrews 7: 22, 8: 6, 7.

[113] Hebrews 7: 12, Romans 10: 4, Romans 7: 4, 6, Galatians 2: 19, 20, 21.

[114] Romans 6: 10.

[115] Galatians 3: 10.

[116] Galatians 3: 13.

[117] 2 Corinthians 3: 6.

[118] Romans 7: 1-4.

[119] Galatians 5: 14.

[120] George Maloney, *The Mystery of Christ in You: The Mystical Vision of Saint Paul* (New York: Alba House, 1998), 31.

[121] Thomas Merton, *The New Man* (New York, NY: Farrar, Straus, & Cudahy, 1961), 167.

[122] Parallel Bible, *Hebrew Lexicon;* http://strongsnumbers.com/hebrew/6213a.htm.

[123] Galatians 2: 20.

[124] Galatians 2: 17, 5: 1.

[125] 2 Corinthians 3: 17.

Chapter 6: Focus

[126] Luke 10: 42.

[127] Underhill, Evelyn. *Practical Mysticism: A Little Book for Normal People* (Columbus, OH: Ariel Press, 1986), 27, 28.

[128] Galatians 2: 17-19.

[129] Titus 2: 11-12, Romans 6: 10.

[130] Romans 8: 1.

[131] Henri J. M. Nouwen, *Here and Now; Living in the Spirit* (New York, NY: Crossroad Publishing Company, 1994), 19.

[132] Evelyn Underhill, *Mysticism: A Study in the Nature and Development of Man's Spiritual Consciousness* (New York, NY E. P. Dutton, 1912), 447.

[133] Francois Fenelon, *The Seeking Heart* (Sargent, GA: The Seedsowers, 1962), 65.

[134] Matthew 6: 33.

[135] Matthew 6: 34.

[136] Matthew 6: 25-34.

Chapter 7: Challenge

[137] Web MD, http://www.webmd.com/depression/guide/exercise-depression (accessed October 28, 2010).

[138] John 13: 34.

[139] Grace Jantzen, *Julian of Norwich: Mystic and Theologian* (New York, NY: Paulist Press, 2000), 93.

[140] Dan Stone and Greg Smith, *The Rest of the Gospel* (Dallas, TX: One Press, 2000), 85.

[141] Parallel Bible, *Greek Lexicon; love,* http://strongsnumbers.com/greek/25.htm.

[142] Luke 10: 25-37.

[143] John 12: 25.

[144] Csikszentmihalyi, *Flow,* 21, 149, 214, 217.

[145] Ibid, 74, 75.

[146] Psalm 16: 5.

[147] Jean Pierre De Caussade, *Abandonment to Divine Providence* (New York: Image Books, 1975), 55.

[148] Jeanne Guyon, *Experiencing the Depths of Jesus Christ* (Sargent, GA: SeedSowers, 1975), 56.

Chapter 8: Feedback

[149] Henri J. M. Nouwen, *Life of the Beloved* (New York, NY: Crossroad, 2000), 26, 28.

[150] 2 Peter 1: 3.

[151] John 14:26, John 15:26.

[152] Canby Jones, ed. *The Power of the Lord Is Over All* (Richmond, IN Friends United Press, 1989), xxiii.

[153] Acts 17:28, John 6: 45.

[154] Matthew 4: 4.

[155] John 12: 49.

[156] John 3: 5-8.

[157] John 14: 26, 15: 26, 16: 13.

[158] Donald Miller, *Blue Like Jazz: Nonreligious Thoughts on Christian Spirituality* (Nashville, TN: Thomas Nelson Publishers, 2003), ix, x.

[159] Ibid, 239.

[160] Ibid.

[161] Philippians 2: 13.

[162] John 15: 5.

[163] Parallel Bible, *Greek Lexicon, abide,* http://strongsnumbers.com/greek/3306.htmJohn 15:5.

[164] Wendy Wright, *Frances de Sales: Introduction to the Devout Life and Treatise on the Love of God* (New York, NY: Crossroad Publishing Company1993), 44.

[165] David Augsburger, *Dissident Discipleship: A Spirituality of Self-Surrender, Love of God, and Love of Neighbor* (Grand Rapids, MI: Brazos Press, 2006), 13.

Chapter 9: The Inward Fruits

[166] Galatians 5: 16-25.

[167] John 15: 5.

[168] More information about Roger's work is available at info@rogerbalko.com.

169 Thomas Merton, *New Seeds of Contemplation* (New York: New Directions Books, 1972), 31.

170 John 14: 27, 20: 19.

171 Parallel Bible, *Greek Lexicon, joy,* http://strongsnumbers.com/greek/5479.htm.

172 Philippians 4: 6, 7.

173 Psalm 46: 10.

174 Henri J. M. Nouwen, *Life of the Beloved,* 26. See also Henri J. M. Nouwen, *Spiritual Direction: Wisdom for the Long Walk of Faith,* ed. M.J. Christensen and R.J. Laird (New York, NY: HarperSanFrancisco, 2007), 29.

175 Francois Fenelon, *The Seeking Heart,* 14.

176 Titus 2: 8-10.

177 Romans 5: 20, 7: 8-11.

178 Matthew 6: 22-33.

Chapter 10: The Outward Fruits

179 Romans 8: 28.

180 Richard Rohr, Andreas Ebert, and Peter Heinegg, *The Enneagram: A Christian Perspective* (New York: Crossroad Pub., 2001), 34.

181 John 14: 10.

182 The film is entitled *Most.* More information can be found at www.mostthemovie.com.

183 Colossians 1: 29.

184 Parallel Bible, *Greek Lexicon; strengthen,* http://strongsnumbers.com/greek/1743.htm. Meyers, *e-Sword,* Philippians 4:13.

185 Gerald May, M.D., *Will and Spirit: A Contemplative Psychology.* (New York, NY: HarperSanFrancisco, 1982), 5-7.

Chapter 11: Flow-Ready Faith

186 Bonnie Thurston, ed. *Merton & Buddhism; Wisdom, Emptiness, & Everyday Mind* (Louisville, KY: Fons Vitae, 2007), 23.

187 Mind, http://dictionary.reference.com/browse/mind (accessed April 16, 2008).

[188] Set, http://dictionary.reference.com/browse/mind (accessed April 16, 2008).

[189] Csikszentmihalyi, *Flow*, 240.

[190] 1 Corinthians 2: 16.

[191] Parallel Bible, *Greek Lexicon; mind*, http://strongsnumbers.com/greek/3563.htm.

[192] Csikszentmihalyi, *Flow*, 5.

[193] 2 Corinthians 10: 5.

[194] Philippians 4: 8.

[195] Gerald May, *Addiction & Grace: Love and Spirituality in the Healing of Addictions* (New York, NY: HarperSanFrancisco, 1988), 58-90.

[196] Romans 12: 2.

[197] Tony Horsfall, *Rhythms of Grace: Finding Intimacy with God in a Busy Life* (Eastbourne, UK: Kingsway Publications, 2004), 16.

[198] Romans 14: 23.

[199] Horsfall, *Rhythms of Grace*, 101.

[200] Anthony Campolo and Mary Darling, *The God of Intimacy and Action; Reconnecting Ancient Spiritual Practices, Evangelism, and Justice* (San Francisco, CA: Jossey-Bass, 2007), 6.

[201] Henri J.M. Nouwen with Michael J. Christensen, and Rebecca Laird, *Spiritual Direction: Wisdom for the Long Walk of Faith* (New York, NY: HarperSanFrancisco, 2006), xvi.

[202] Thomas Merton, *Thoughts in Solitude* (Boston, MA: Shambhala, 1993), 3.

[203] Reggie McNeal, *Practicing Greatness; 7 Disciplines of Extraordinary Spiritual Leaders*. 2006 (San Francisco, CA Jossey-Bass, 2006), 63.

[204] Philippians 2: 7.

[205] Luke 9: 23.

[206] Genesis 22, Luke 1: 38, Luke 22: 42.

Chapter 12: Living Into the Sacred Flow

[207] Parallel Bible, *Greek Lexicon; idolatry*, http://strongsnumbers.com/greek/1495.htm.

[208] Dietrich Bonhoeffer, *The Cost of Discipleship* (New York, NY: Macmillan Publishing Co., 1963), 205.

[209] Galatians 3:26, Romans 8:14-17.

[210] Peter Scazzero, *Emotionally Healthy Spirituality* (Nashville, TN: Integrity Publishers, 2006), 54.

[211] *The Legend of Bagger Vance*, directed by Robert Redford, Dreamworks, 2000.

[212] John 17: 18.

[213] Luke 4: 18-19.

Appendix: Practicing Grace

[214] Henri J. M. Nouwen, *Here and Now; Living in the Spirit* (New York, NY: Crossroad Publishing Company, 1994), 23.

[215] Richard Foster, *Prayer: Finding the Heart's True Home* (New York, NY: HarperSanFrancisco, 1992), 9.

[216] Henri J. M. Nouwen, *The Way of the Heart* (New York, NY: Ballantine Books, 1981), 40.

[217] Ibid, 13.

[218] Richard Foster, *Celebration of Discipline; The Path to Spiritual Growth* (SanFrancisco, CA: HarperSanFrancisco, 1988), 96.

[219] Thomas Keating, Thomas *Open Mind Open Heart: The Contemplative Dimension of the Gospel* (New York, NY: Continuum, 1997), 43.

[220] Bernadette Dieker and Jonathan Montaldo, eds. *Merton & Hesychasm: The Prayer of the Heart* (Fons Vitae: Louisville, KY, 2003), 11.

[221] Alan Wallace, *The Attention Revolution: Unlocking the Power of the Focused Mind* (Boston, MA: Wisdom Publications, 2006), 32.

[222] James Finley, *Christian Meditation; Experiencing the Presence of God* (San Francisco, CA: HarperSanFrancisco, 2004), 7.

[223] Tom Francis explains that the term *centering prayer* was birthed as a way to de-mystify and de-clergify contemplation. Tom Francis, *Contemplative Prayer* (Conyers, GA: Monastery of the Holy Spirit, 2008).

[224] Fr. Michael, *Lectio Divina* (Conyers, GA: Monastery of the Holy Spirit, 2008).

[225] William Johnston, *Mystical Theology: The Science of Love* (Maryknoll, NY: Orbis Books, 1995), 3.

[226] Richard Foster, *Celebration of Discipline*, 65.

[227] John 4: 24.

[228] David G. Benner, *Sacred Companions: The Gift of Spiritual Friendship & Direction* (Downers Grove, IL: InterVarsity Press, 2002), 15.

[229] Jim Loehr and Tony Schwartz. *The Power of Full Engagement*, 5.

[230] Hebrews 4: 9-11.

To order more books or
for more information go to:

www.thesacredflow.com

CPSIA information can be obtained at www.ICGtesting.com
Printed in the USA
LVOW042128141211

259485LV00001B/6/P